"This is unlike any book I have ever read. Seth is a great writer, and this work of poetic theology is as beautiful as it is faithful. It has impacted me to the extent that even walking in the park is a new experience—one of awe and wonder."

ALISTAIR BEGG, Bible Teacher, *Truth for Life*

"With the heart of a poet and the hand of a novelist, Seth beautifully describes all that becomes too easily obscured when it comes to the mystery and majesty of nature. Prepare to be captivated anew by the profundity of God's glory reflected through his magnificent creation. Enlighten and delight your mind!"

RONNIE MARTIN, Director of Leader Care & Renewal, Harbor Network; Co-Author, *The Unhurried Pastor*

"Theology, nature, wonder and creativity are woven together into this beautifully written work of art. Infused with worship, Christ-centred and thoroughly biblical, this book inspires you to worship as you wander through creation, to see more than you've ever seen and to learn to respond, 'Wow!' This is undoubtedly one of the best Christian books I've read; I loved every word."

LINDA ALLCOCK, Author, *Deeper Still*

"This beautiful book takes us on a journey of discovering, interpreting and ultimately responding to God's marvellous communication in the natural world. Seth Lewis's language is often enchanting, but his main goal is to invite each of us into relationship with the greatest wonder of all: creation's author. This is winsome work—evocative, personal, well-informed and compelling. Writing at its best."

SHARON JONES, Lecturer, Stranmillis University College, and Belfast School of Theology

"In the busyness of life, we often sadly turn in on ourselves and forget to pause, observe the beauty of creation around us, and, most importantly, understand that the entire creation, even in a post-fall world, bears witness to the existence, glory and wonder of our glorious triune God. Seth Lewis's book is a wonderful reminder to stop, look, reflect on what we often take for granted and rightly see that the heavens declare God's glory if we will only listen. This is a wonderfully written book that reminds us that we cannot escape the God who has made us and that true enjoyment comes in knowing him, not only through what he has made but ultimately in the glory of our Lord Jesus Christ. Take up and read, and learn to enjoy the beauty of God's creation and new creation in Christ. I highly recommend this book."

STEPHEN J. WELLUM, Professor of Christian Theology, The Southern Baptist Theological Seminary

"I often feel closer to God when walking in a wood than sitting in church and have wondered whether I am a secret pagan! *The Language of Rivers and Stars* has put such fears to rest. Using the seven days of creation as his framework, Seth explores how we can read the book of nature, so that light and sun, sky and sea, the earth beneath our feet and the star-filled sky at night, the rhythms of the seasons and the wonderful profusion of plants, animals and our human selves that fill our planet all speak to us of the glories of God. This book is a delight from start to finish and has encouraged me to look more carefully, listen more quietly, wonder more deeply and care more lovingly for this beautiful world that points to its amazing Creator God."

JAMES PAUL, Director, English branch of L'Abri Fellowship; Author, *What on Earth Is Heaven?*

SETH LEWIS

THE

LANGUAGE

OF

RIVERS

AND

STARS

HOW NATURE SPEAKS OF
THE GLORIES OF GOD

The Language of Rivers and Stars
How Nature Speaks of the Glories of God

© Seth Lewis, 2025

Published by:
The Good Book Company

thegoodbook.com | thegoodbook.co.uk
thegoodbook.com.au | thegoodbook.co.nz | thegoodbook.co.in

Cover design by The Good Book Company.

ISBN: 9781802542967 | JOB-008068 | Printed in India

To Jessica,
who makes the world bloom.

Contents

Introduction: The Language of Creation   9

Part I: Everything Speaks

  1. The Sun-Disc   19

  2. The Rosetta Stone   27

  3. Glories and Groans   37

  4. The Art of Interpretation   47

Part II: To Hear and Respond

  5. Let There Be Light   59

  6. A Never-Ending Newsfeed   67

  7. The Chaos Container   75

  8. The Clay and the Potter   83

  9. The Seeds of Life   91

  10. The Rhythm of Time   99

  11. Naming the Stars   107

  12. The Mysteries of the Deep   115

13. The Freedom of the Skies   123

14. More Than Meets the Eye   131

15. The Image of God   139

16. The Rest of the Story   147

17. I Wonder as I Wander   155

The Language of Creation

It was the middle of the night, in the middle of nowhere. There must have been clouds above us because, beyond our headlights, the darkness was complete. The only sound was the crunch of gravel under our tyres as we pulled into a wide spot beside a lake we could not yet see. I cut the engine off, and all was calm.

The only thing that disturbed the peace was my wife and I opening and closing doors, and preparing our kayak. With the help of our phone torches we found the lake and launched ourselves onto it. That's when the magic began.

This is what we had come for. We had heard many stories about Lough Hyne. And today was the day we'd finally got a babysitter, borrowed a kayak, stayed up and driven out. We did all of this for a sight we were not entirely sure we would even see, and if we did see it, we weren't entirely sure it would be as magical as we were led to believe.

But it was. As the kayak floated away from the launch ramp, we put our paddles into the still, dark water, and the still, dark water immediately exploded with light. Every stroke created new fireworks in the water—a thousand glimmers for every touch, radiating out in sparkling ripples before fading away. I realise this sounds hard to believe. We could barely believe it ourselves. The sparks were not actually fireworks or some kind of man-made concoction; they were living organisms. The enchanted lake was filled with bioluminescent plankton—microscopic creatures too small to see with the naked eye, yet when they are disturbed, a chemical reaction within their tiny bodies creates a bright blue light. The lake really was alive with beauty.

We didn't go far. Why would we? Our eyes don't work well in the dark. The only reason we didn't run into a boulder was because at the last minute we noticed that the blackness was a shade blacker there. We paddled in circles, and we did it happily, splashing up a sea of starlight. I was so enthralled at what was happening under the surface that I didn't notice the sky clearing until Jessica said, "Look up!" Sure enough, there were millions—no—billions of stars above us, clusters and constellations so far beyond counting, and all of them sharing their light with two tiny people in a tiny boat on an enchanted lake in a hidden little corner of Ireland. We were surrounded. Speechless. Overwhelmed. Stars above, stars below. Magic. Awe. Wonder.

There are scientific explanations for what Jessica and I saw that night—for the plasma blazing in the sky and the plankton sparking in the water. Humans have researched these things. We have classified them and categorised them and published papers on how we can predict and understand them. We have microscopes and telescopes. Even I, with only my introductory science classes that were so many years ago, know I'm looking at cells and gases; but my knowledge doesn't change anything—it's still magical.

The Language of Stars Is Not Latin

How does the world do this to us? How does it make our hearts beat faster and our eyes go wide and our minds freeze, transfixed with beauty? How do pinpricks of burning gas and glowing biology (and so many other natural realities) have such strange power over us? Is this really logical? Our long, impressive scientific names are not long or impressive enough to capture the long-term impression these spectacles make on us. The stars don't use our carefully chosen words. You'll never understand them with the language of science alone.

There is no survival value in gaping at the midnight sky. My wife and I lost half a night's sleep and almost hit a boulder on that lake. But we were gaping anyway, and loving it—just as every other human who ever lived on this planet has gaped at the world and loved its beauty. Our ancestors worshipped the stars as gods and believed the woods were teeming with faeries. I don't agree with them, but I understand why. The magic is real, with or without the faeries. It's real, with or without the formulas.

Scientific methods can be useful, in fairness. Our understanding of the world has made us comfortable, helping us harness nature and direct it. Many of us don't live in caves or huts or even cold stone castles anymore.

Now in the West we have insulated walls that shelter climate-controlled rooms with light switches and hot-water supplies and sockets that channel electricity into user-friendly labour-saving and entertainment devices. Inside these walls, the world works the way I want it to, and everything is made to the scale of me—the bed, the refrigerator, the couch, the doorway, the ceiling, and the screen that is smart enough to show me my interests before I tell it to (a bit scary, that). But being able to control my living environment almost completely hasn't completed my experience of living. We can sit inside and make ourselves the right temperature and make our food the right temperature and feed our brains with all of the accumulated knowledge and funny cat videos of human civilisation, and even with all of this at our literal fingertips, we are still restless and discontented. We have mastered the world, but we haven't figured out what to do with it yet. So we watch another cat video.

I've seen my share of funny videos, and I've laughed along and learned plenty of interesting things online, but I've never seen anything on a screen that made me feel as vitally alive as being on a glowing lake at midnight with my wife. This is not an anomaly—as I look back on the favourite memories that I've accumulated through my few decades of living, I find that hardly any of them have anything to do with screens and very few with couches, and a disproportionate number of them have occurred outdoors. Beaches. Forests. Picnics. Campgrounds. Mountains. Cliffs. Islands. Stars. Water. Fire. Why is the highlight reel of my life so dominated by memories in places that are not nearly as comfortable as my couch? Why does sitting on a beach make me forget about the technology in my pocket that can speak to me in my own native tongue, answer my questions, show me directions, give me recommendations and carry out my commands? I'd rather listen to the waves. I like their language better.

Speaking with Mountains

I went up a mountain with some friends from church—the tallest mountain in Ireland in fact. Our legs hurt. The rough wind took our breath away. Stephen's hands went numb. Jonathan's shoes fell apart. A streaky drizzle soaked us all, and we loved it. Seriously, I loved it. I felt so alive, so aware. I felt all of my senses working and my muscles working and my mind working, and I couldn't keep myself from smiling as I walked through the rain and the pain—not in spite of the work and miserable conditions but because of them. Nothing on that mountain was my size. Not the clouds, not the boulders, not the mountain itself or the wild landscape stretching out from it as far as I could see. I couldn't flip a switch and control it. I couldn't close a window or draw a curtain or change the channel. I couldn't even yell, "Hey mountain" and get it to play some rainy-day mood music for me.

Not that I wanted to. Music couldn't have made my mood better, anyway. I didn't care about my soggy, heavy jeans. I didn't care that the guys said, "You're brave to wear jeans"—or that it was nice of them to substitute "brave" for "foolish". I didn't care that I felt unfit, panting and struggling to keep putting one foot in front of the other. Out of shape or not, I was alive. I could climb a mountain. I could make it to the top, and back again. This was not a given—the boulders were wet, and the way was steep. Someone in a group in front of us slipped and landed head first on the rocks at the feet of a man who happened to be a doctor. I don't know if he felt lucky or unlucky about that, but I bet he did feel alive and thankful. That mountain was uncomfortable, unsafe and unforgettable. Even the difficulty and danger spoke to us.

How does the outdoors move us so deeply and have such power to make us feel more alive, more connected, more rested and content than any technology or device we've been able to invent—even though it is so often wild, unpredictable and threatening? Nature stirs us with sunsets, calms us with steady waves and terrifies us with power. We hear it. We feel it. We sense it communicating, and something inside of us responds naturally. Innately. Even if we don't understand the language. This conversation—between us and the world—happens whether we want it to or not.

The Speaking and the Speaker

We are unique this way. The animals may be more in tune with nature than we will ever be, but they don't appreciate it like we do. Some of them are instinctually guided by the light of the moon, but they don't write poetry about it. They don't try to read fortunes in the movements of constellations and planets or paint starry, starry nights in order to capture and share the emotions they experienced when they saw them in person. Humanity alone is haunted by this powerful feeling that the world is speaking something deeply meaningful to us. And there's a reason why we feel this: it *is*.

For the director of music. A psalm of David.

The heavens declare the glory of God;
the skies proclaim the work of his hands.
Day after day they pour forth speech;
night after night they reveal knowledge.
They have no speech, they use no words;
no sound is heard from them.
Yet their voice goes out into all the earth,
their words to the ends of the world. (Psalm 19:1-4)

Have you ever considered that the reason why we feel so connected in nature is because that's what nature is specifically designed to do? It is made to connect us to our Maker. It doesn't use words, but it still communicates. Powerfully. It declares, proclaims, reveals and speaks to the ends of the earth—because there isn't one tiny corner of this planet that isn't filled up and overflowing with God's creative wonders. And the wonder that we naturally feel in response to his wonders is not an accident of our genetics. It is not some kind of sentimentality that only holds us back from being as ruthlessly efficient as we could be in our quest to survive. Our wonder is the natural language of our created souls responding to the natural language of our created world.

Speaking requires a speaker: for communication to happen, there must be someone with a message to communicate. If there is proclamation, declaration and revelation, there must be something to proclaim, something to declare—someone to reveal. "The heavens declare the glory of God" (v 1)—the language of creation is more than a lovely feeling. It is real language, with real meaning, direction and intention. It is telling us truth we really need to know. But how do we understand a language with no words? How do we listen to the one who is speaking to us through it?

Thankfully, the God who speaks to us through his world has also given us everything we need to interpret his meaning. In the following chapters, we will consider how we can hear our Creator's voice in his creation; not only to understand clearly what he is saying to us, but also—vitally—to respond. Then, in Part II, we will use the days of creation as a path to begin a journey of listening and responding to God's voice in all his natural wonders—because everything God made is speaking to us, every day.

PART I

Everything Speaks

CHAPTER 1

The Sun-Disc

"Nature gave the word 'glory' a meaning for me. I still do not know where else I could have found one."

C.S. Lewis

On the banks of the River Nile, the temple of Amun-Re still stands proud, with stone walls and statues carved by human hands that have long since returned to the dust from which they came. Rows of towering pillars stand open to the blazing sun, now holding up nothing but the memory of a glorious civilisation. Each pillar is covered with chiselled pictures of people, animals, objects and shapes—hieroglyphics, the sacred writing of ancient Egypt.

For centuries, the knowledge of how to interpret this writing was buried with the last of the priests and pharaohs, inaccessible to us inside the minds of mummies. But the writing itself remained, carved in stone, monumental and mysterious. Even without a translation, one thing is clear to every awed observer:

the language of ancient Egypt was built on the realities of the natural world. You don't have to know how to read hieroglyphics to recognise the form of a man, a beetle or a hawk. On the temples of ancient Egypt, these images were used to communicate meaning. And given the climate of Egypt, it is not surprising that one symbol of particular importance was a circle—sometimes with rays, sometimes with wings, sometimes with only a dot in the middle—representing the sun. On its own, this carved sun-disc could be used to communicate the passage of time or the shining of light. With wings, it could represent the entire land of Egypt. With rays, it could denote divinity, royalty and power.

The sun was important to ancient Egyptians, and it's not hard to see why. For all that has changed in the last few thousand years, our dependence on the sun has not. How could we live without it? When it comes to raw power and the provision of life, warmth and light, the sun reigns supreme—for the whole world, for all of history.

A Higher Hieroglyph

Far above the temple of Amun-Re, the sun-disc that inspired all these Egyptian drawings blazes down from the vast expanse of God's sky. Along with every other star, it is a kind of hieroglyph, created to communicate. Even the sky itself is a message. As we've already seen in Psalm 19, King David writes:

The heavens declare the glory of God;
the skies proclaim the work of his hands.

Day after day they pour forth speech;
  night after night they reveal knowledge.
They have no speech, they use no words;
  no sound is heard from them.
Yet their voice goes out into all the earth,
  their words to the ends of the world.   *(v 1-4)*

As David looked up, he saw a message. He heard a declaration of God's glory as he viewed the things God had made. He recognised that the whole world—the whole universe—is speaking to us constantly with a wordless voice that never stops pouring forth speech and revealing knowledge. And if you've ever looked up at the sky as David did, you'll know that nothing in all the heavens speaks more powerfully than the sun:

In the heavens God has pitched a tent for the sun.
It is like a bridegroom coming out of his chamber,
  like a champion rejoicing to run his course.
It rises at one end of the heavens
  and makes its circuit to the other;
  nothing is deprived of its warmth.   *(v 4-6)*

Perhaps this feels like a digression. In the earlier verses he was making a clear point: the heavens speak to us about God's glory. But what's all this about the sun having a tent, getting married and running races?

First, it's poetry. It's meant to move you, to make you feel something, and is there a stronger feeling of joy than the joy of a bridegroom on his wedding day? He beams—and so does the sun: it's vital and hot; it's awesomely powerful, blazing across the sky like a champion racer who runs with complete confidence and never fears loss, never holds back, but burns every muscle in pushing forward.

Second, it's not just poetry. The words used are an attempt to capture in language a small part of what the sun is saying to us every day. The warmth it gives, the path it follows, the sky-tent it lives in—it all means something; it all says something. Even when you're inside, it reaches out to you and speaks to you through the windows, and it's okay to close your eyes and lean into its light as the houseplants do. All night long there are billions of stars in the sky, singing together in their silent chorus—but then every morning, our friendly local star comes centre stage for his daily solo. "The heavens declare the glory of God", and the sun in all his shining glory is no exception; his path is set by God. His tent is pitched by God. The sun *is* God's work and *does* God's work. The power of the sun displays the power of the sun's Maker. It is God's power. His warmth is God's warmth. The joyful daily race he runs is God's joyful daily care for his world.

The Language of Reality

Did God have to make a sun to say these things to us? He could have started speaking to us only with words like "I am powerful, and I can provide for you"—and those words would have been just as true. But then how would we know what the words meant without some kind of real, tangible experience of power and provision? What is power? What is provision? By making a sun for us, God gave us the ability to understand what he means when he says these words.

With a sun above us, we immediately recognise the realities that those words represent. We see real power in the sky. We feel it on our skin. We watch the daily provision of warmth and light bring life and joy to the world. The truth of God's character and his words is made tangible to us. Before God communicated to us in our language of words, he first had to communicate to us in his language of realities. His language is what makes our language possible. He had to establish the realities first, and only after that was he free to begin describing them to us with the verbal language we're used to.

Now that literacy rates are so high and technology is so developed, we are immersed in a constant stream of talking and writing and reading and listening and video chatting across the globe. And yet I wonder if, in all our word-sharing, perhaps we've forgotten what our words actually are. Let's step back a moment and remember: our language is not equal to God's. When God made the world, he did it by speaking: "Let there be" (Genesis 1:3), and there was. So God's language is creative—he speaks existence. He says, "Light," and there is light. Not the idea of light but the physical reality itself. His word for light is not spelled in letters like L I G H T. It is spelled in burning suns and lightning and the backsides of fireflies. His word for "light" is light itself. His word for "fish" has scales and squirms in the water. His word for "mountain" towers over our heads. His language is not like ours.

Our language is descriptive, not creative. We do not use it to invent realities but only as a way to speak about them. The ancient Egyptians called their hieroglyphic writing "god's words" and covered their temples with images of God's realities, but their pictures were only pictures—their birds were recognisable, but they did not fly. Their sun was the right shape, but it gave no heat. Our words are the same. Our word for "warmth" conveys the concept of a feeling we all recognise—the feeling of being warm. But if you're cold, it won't matter how many times I say (or even shout) the word "warmth" to you. You'll still be cold. Sorry. Maybe grab a blanket instead. Our words can convey ideas and concepts and mental pictures and feelings and all sorts of things—it really is marvellous what words can describe. (I'm doing it right now, in fact, and you are reading meaning out of these little squiggly ink lines, which is kind of crazy if you think about it.) But as amazing as our words are, they have their limitations. They can only describe reality; they cannot physically create it.

The Purpose of Language

That's okay—God has already taken care of the creating part. But he left most of the describing to us, and he gifted us the ability to do it by giving us words. This is not an accident or an afterthought. The gift of language speaks to one of our roles in the world God made for us; we are the voice of creation. The heavens declare, but the heavens have no words. We do. We hear their declaration and provide the words for them. We listen to reality and are able to describe it. We have the ability to respond to what we see.

And who are we responding to? The artist, that's who. The one who carved and painted and planted this world gave it to us as a gift—not just a painting we could hang up in our home but an entire living art gallery that we could make our home. That's quite a gift. But if you've ever been to an art gallery, you know that art is not created to merely exist. It is created to communicate. It might communicate an idea or a feeling or a call to action, but it always communicates something. It pours forth speech, even though it uses no words, and that silent speech is heavy with a message from the artist. Art is specifically created to speak to us in the language of colours, textures, carved stones and captured scenes. And it works: "A picture is worth a thousand words".

So it is with our world. It does not merely exist as a life-support machine to enable our existence. It is a message. It is the art gallery of reality, speaking as loudly as possible in the language of colours, textures, ancient stones and living scenes. It is the pillar room in the temple of Amun-Re, covered with pictorial language—a sacred language, telling a sacred story, pointing beyond itself to sacred realities. God's language is deep. And just as the Egyptians did not carve their circles simply for us to admire their roundness, God did not light his sun simply for us to admire its brightness. The sun is one of his hieroglyphs—one massive, burning ball of meaning. He hung it in the sky as a picture, worth so many thousands of words, to point beyond itself and make sure we had a context to better understand and better respond to the most important reality in the universe: himself. "The heavens declare the glory of

God"—when we see the sun, we see a glimpse of God's power. When it lights and warms us and makes our world bloom and grow, we see a demonstration of his care and provision for us.

The meaning is there, already built in. But deciphering hieroglyphics isn't always easy. The ancient Egyptians saw the same sun we see today, but they interpreted its meaning differently: they did not see beyond the picture to the artist who created it. They did not let the picture point them to God. They decided the picture was itself a god. Even God's hieroglyphics can be misread. How can we be sure that we are reading them rightly?

CHAPTER 2

The Rosetta Stone

"God has two textbooks, Scripture and creation. We would do well to listen to both."

Francis Bacon

I don't know anyone who cares about the great deeds of Ptolemy V anymore. I don't think anyone anywhere believes that he was the divine son of a sun-god. No one went looking for a declaration of his greatness—but we have one. It was discovered accidentally in 1799 by soldiers in Napoleon's army, who were stationed in a town called Rosetta. Did they know that their "Rosetta Stone" would become the key that unlocked the lost language of ancient Egypt?

The reason why people know how to read Egyptian hieroglyphics today is because a council of priests carved the same message in two languages—Egyptian and Greek—on the same stone 196 years before the birth of Jesus. When the Rosetta Stone was found, no one living could read hieroglyphics, but plenty of people could read Greek. By working back from the known language, the meaning of the unknown language became clear. Now, people can once again read the pillars in the temple of Amun-Re, along with all the hieroglyphics of Egypt.

Before this discovery, scholars had worked hard at guessing the meaning of what the Egyptians had written. Some guesses were completely wrong, while others were surprisingly accurate. Either way, they were guesses. Who could say for sure who was right and who was wrong? But now, thanks to the Rosetta Stone, we know exactly what those once-mysterious pictures mean. We have a standard to evaluate our guesses by. Better—we don't need to guess at all.

A Rosetta Stone for Nature

Is it possible to look at nature's hieroglyphs, like the sun blazing away in the midday sky, and learn to read meaning clearly from them—beyond our own gut feelings and personal preferences? For this to be possible, we would need a trustworthy translation key. We would need a Rosetta Stone for nature: something written in a language we already know, by the same author, with the same message as the natural pictures we see around us. Do we have such a key? We do.

Remember how David celebrated how creation communicates in Psalm 19, and then highlighted its most prominent character, the sun? That's not the end of his psalm. David has more to say. The following verses may seem like a change of topic from what came before,

but they are not. They are only the other half of the
Rosetta Stone—the one in a language we already know:

> *The law of the LORD is perfect,*
>   *refreshing the soul.*
> *The statutes of the LORD are trustworthy,*
>   *making wise the simple.*
> *The precepts of the LORD are right,*
>   *giving joy to the heart.*
> *The commands of the LORD are radiant,*
>   *giving light to the eyes.*
> *The fear of the LORD is pure,*
>   *enduring for ever.*
> *The decrees of the LORD are firm,*
>   *and all of them are righteous.*   *(v 7-9)*

David is talking about God's written word, the Bible.
When he read Scripture, he recognised that the voice
behind its words was the same voice that was pouring
forth speech from all of creation (v 2). The difference is
that the Bible is written in the kind of words we're used
to using ourselves. It is the Greek on the Rosetta Stone,
speaking to us in familiar terms we already know how
to interpret. And what are the terms saying? The words
of Scripture point us back to the God who wrote them.
God's commands are "perfect", "trustworthy", "right",
"radiant" and "pure" because the God who gave them
is all of those things. David had seen the radiant light
of the sun, and now he saw that the "commands of the
Lord are radiant, giving light to the eyes." He had seen
the sun rise faithfully every morning, and he knew that
he could trust the statutes of the Lord, which came from

the same source. He had felt the sun's refreshing warmth, and his soul was refreshed in the law of the Lord. The world around him helped him understand something of the meaning of Scripture, and the words of Scripture help him understand the message of creation. David saw that both languages were pointing him in the same direction, sharing the same truths about the same God through different media. The wordless communication of nature gave him the context he needed to understand the even greater revelation of God's word. Look at how he carries on from verse 10, still extolling God's decrees:

> *They are more precious than gold,*
> *than much pure gold;*
> *they are sweeter than honey,*
> *than honey from the honeycomb.* (v 10)

The value of glittering gold is a picture—a hieroglyph that teaches us what "precious" means so that we can recognise the greater value of God's words, which are more precious than "much pure gold". The sweet taste of honey is a gift that our taste buds are designed to enjoy: a gift designed to give us a taste for the joy found in the even sweeter reality of the God who invented both the honey and the taste buds that enjoy it. God is the one who painted these natural pictures for us. They are his letters and lines, heavy with meaning. So if that same writer also wrote to us in our own native tongue, wouldn't we want to read his message? Wouldn't we long with all our hearts to hear what the Maker of all of these astounding natural realities has to say to us in our own language? That's how David felt about it.

David loves God's words because they reveal to him the nature of the God behind those words and help him respond rightly to him. It's for the same reason that David loves God's world—because it reveals the God behind the world. In Psalm 19, he rejoices in both languages, and how they reveal the same God. "The heavens declare the glory of God"—and what is it that the Bible does? It also declares the glory of God. It *pours forth speech* and *reveals knowledge* through its words. These are two languages with one message, pointing in one direction: to our Creator.

God's Voice and Ours

In Psalm 19, David's interest in God is not merely academic, for answering questions or filing facts away in his brain. He does not want to know what God says simply for the novelty of hearing from him. It's personal: he hears God speaking to him, and he wants to know how to respond. He wants to know how to relate to this Creator God, who made him and communicates to him constantly in his world and his word. That's why David ends this psalm the way he does, still revelling in the joy of being given words from the God of everything:

By them your servant is warned;
    in keeping them there is great reward.
But who can discern their own errors?
    Forgive my hidden faults.
Keep your servant also from wilful sins;
    may they not rule over me.
Then I will be blameless,
    innocent of great transgression.

> *May these words of my mouth and this meditation*
>   *of my heart*
>   *be pleasing in your sight,*
>   LORD, *my Rock and my Redeemer.*   *(v 11-14)*

Notice how David ends his psalm about God's words with a prayer about his own. After deeply considering God's voice in creation and Scripture, his great concern is to respond with his own voice in a truly appropriate way. When he reflects on the greatness of the God who is speaking to him, he feels keenly his own faults, weaknesses and sins. But he approaches anyway, praying for God's forgiveness and help to respond rightly. What we see here is that David is not only hearing the *what* of God's communication but the *why*. Why does the God of everything condescend to communicate with humans? Why does he write his messages in the sweeping hieroglyphics of creation and then write them again in the lines of Scripture?

Before we even begin to interpret the specifics of what God says, the fact that he communicates with us at all tells us something important. Communication is relational. God did not have to speak to us. He communicates because he wants to reveal himself. He gave us his word and his world to invite us to know and relate to him. He gave this invitation in two languages, and the completeness and clarity of the language of Scripture has not diminished our need to hear God's voice in his creation as well. Scripture itself is filled with references to God's world—from mountains and stars to sparrows and wild flowers and the morning mist that evaporates in the rising sunshine. God never intended for us to choose one language and ignore the other. In Psalm 19, David hears God's invitation in both languages, and he responds with communication of his own. This is how relationships work. Communication calls for response. God's word does not simply inform us about God; it invites us to respond to him. And the whole world around us calls for the same response. Don't you feel that call when you go outside? I do.

The Call of Creation

When I was small, our family built a log home in the rolling hills of northern Alabama. The locals call the place Possum Holler. That's not a name you'll find on a map, but it's where I grew up, alongside the peach and pecan trees my dad planted in front of the house. Behind it, a forest rises with the mountain. It begins with impossibly tall pine trees swaying in the breeze, but as you climb there are oaks and maples and cedars, stream beds and rock outcroppings. I used to wander there with Cinnamon, our cocker spaniel. She stayed busy sniffing out the scent of every creature that had ever passed by, while I spent the time looking, listening, and praying. I'm sure I looked strange, talking out loud with no one there to talk to, but that's just the point: there was someone to talk to. And everything I saw around me was his work, his language, calling me to respond to him.

That's why for my whole life most of my favourite spots for praying have been outside. There's a large tree on the edge of a university campus in the Blue Ridge Mountains of Virginia that overheard years of my worries and relational troubles. There's a beach on the south coast of Ireland where I wrestled with God and argued and resisted but later came back to thank him for how the waves of his providence had reshaped my heart like the colourful smooth stones that wash up on the shore there.

There's a small graveyard up the hill behind the house we live in now. In the midst of the headstones, there's an ancient yew tree with a view of the entire valley. Beside it stands the last wall of a forgotten church, completely covered in vines. I go there to pray now, like the people who used to go to that church. All through history, people have sought God in the setting of his creation. We can feel more connected to him there. This is no surprise; connecting us to God is exactly what God designed his creation to do. And to make sure we don't miss the meaning of his message to us, he gave us his words as well.

Words in the Garden

When God made Adam and Eve, he put them in a garden and walked there with them every day. Can you imagine what that garden was like? Can you imagine this world when it was fresh and perfect and every plant and creature existed in harmony? It was the perfect setting for humans to meet with God. And when they met together, they spoke. They conversed, in human language, in a garden full of God's wonders. Even in a perfect world, God did not limit himself to speaking through natural pictures alone. He used both languages, and his words to Adam and Eve interpreted for them the meaning of the world he had given them.

God's words guided Adam and Eve in their interaction

with and understanding of his world. His language of realities gave them a context in which to understand his language of words, and his language of words helped them to understand the meaning of his language of realities. Both languages helped them understand and relate to the God who walked with them. The same dynamic is true for us today—God still speaks to us in both languages. He tells us in his word what this world is, what it is for, and how we can read his meaning in it. He calls to us through both languages to know him and respond to him. But things have changed since the garden—we don't walk with God today as our first parents did. Eden is gone. Adam and Eve were expelled from it, into the wilderness, where our human race has lived ever since. If we're going to read the meaning of nature properly, we need to understand this. Our world is glorious, and yet it groans. To interpret it, we must look carefully at what God's word (our Rosetta Stone) says about both the glories and the groans.

CHAPTER 3

Glories and Groans

"I have learned to kiss the wave that throws me against the Rock of Ages."

Attributed to Charles Spurgeon

From the windows of our home in Ireland, we can see beyond the borders of our village to the surrounding hills dotted with sheep and crossed with ancient stone walls now covered with growing hedges. Everything grows here. The vivid greens of the Irish countryside are legendary, a direct result of our legendary rain. Without the rain, Ireland would be an ordinary rock in the sea. With it, we are a shining emerald in a setting of blue. It is a blessing. But not always.

On the 18th of October 2023, our area received a month's worth of rain in 24 hours. A month's worth of Irish rain is a lot. The ground, so green and lush and well watered, refused to take any more. The rivers carried away what they could, but they couldn't carry it fast enough. Their banks broke. The green fields quickly became brown lakes. Then the lakes came into the streets, and the streets became rivers. Then the rivers came up to the doors—and they didn't knock. The entire heart of the town next to us was submerged under several feet of water. Usually, the rain is a blessing. Usually, it brings life and makes our island grow. This time, the rain was too much. It was a curse.

If "the heavens declare the glory of God", then why don't they stop raining before the streets and houses flood? If the earth and everything in it is his handiwork, why do gentle breezes sometimes become destructive hurricanes? Why do healthy cells sometimes become cancer? What is creation saying to us when it includes things like gloriously striped tigers who want to eat us for lunch? A tiger is beautiful but dangerous, like a priceless Monet painted on a bazooka. If we are living in an art gallery, it's a strange one. It has so much life, everywhere you look—trees, rabbits, microbes, songbirds. It has so much death, everywhere you look— spiderwebs, viruses, carcasses, claws. If creation points to its Creator, then how can we know if the God behind this world is more like the rain that makes things grow or the flood that carries them away? Does he walk away from his offspring like an ostrich or spread his wing over us like a hen? Does he stalk us like a tiger or warm us like the sun?

One of the biggest difficulties in interpreting the hieroglyphics of creation is the fact that creation seems to point in two opposite directions at the same time. There is glory, everywhere. But there is also groaning, everywhere. How do we understand these things? This is not the time for guessing. We need the Rosetta Stone of God's word.

True or False

Remember: God does not speak through creation alone. He never has. In the beginning, he gave Adam and Eve a command—with words—about one part of his creation in particular: a tree with fruit. *Don't eat that. Eat all the rest, whatever you like, but don't eat that because, if you do, you will die.* Simple. Clear. An easy, straightforward test with an open book: *will you trust me?* Multiple choice, with two possible answers:

Yes.

No.

It was a simple command with high stakes. A choice to obey would be a choice to remain close to God, in dependence on him. A choice to disobey would be a choice to call him a liar and set out independently, without him. God told them clearly, "When you eat from it you will certainly die" (Genesis 2:16-17). Satan came later and lied to them: "You will not certainly die" (Genesis 3:4). That day, humanity decided that we didn't need to obey God—that we could live without him and remake his world into our own image instead of reflecting his. The rest is history—in all its broken, painful, groaning mess.

God was telling the truth. You can't reject the life-giver and expect to keep the life that only he can give.

"You will certainly die" was a statement of fact, not only a judgment. But somehow, we began to believe that we could do better without him—without having to obey him or depend on him. We walked away from him, and so he purposed that we would take with us the whole creation that he had made us rulers over. We thought we could take his stage and his lights and use the breath that he put in our lungs to speak a better story than he could. We thought we could invent a new truth for ourselves, write a new script, manifest a new destiny. We thought we could overrule God's words with our own. But remember: our language is not like his. He speaks a language of realities; we speak a language of descriptions. Our words cannot re-create his realities, they can only reinterpret them. No matter how elaborate our reinterpretive stories may be (and so often are), the true meaning of reality remains unchanged. No matter how often and loudly and convincingly we talk about not needing God, our world is still dying without him—just as he said it would. He was right. Our new truth is a lie.

A Hopeful Curse

God could have ended everything immediately, right there and then. He could have said to humanity, *You don't want me anymore? Fine. I'll leave you alone. Go and create your own life. You can't have mine anymore.* Drop the curtain; turn off the lights. End of scene. End of story. End of history. Short and not very sweet.

We deserved it. We still do, if we're honest. But God hasn't dropped the curtain. He left the stage lights on and let the play run. He let the drama unfold as a tragedy, with all its beauty and chaos and disorder, life and death and disaster. Instead of ending us, he chose to give us a curse. Yes, I meant to use that word—he *gave* it. Like a gift. I know that sounds backwards. But when the whole world is turned around, sometimes you have to go backwards in order to go forwards. God told Adam and Eve that they would die, and they did die, but not immediately—first, they lived. And in their lives on earth, and in ours today, we now get to taste both good and evil. We get to see the glory of God reflected in all that he made, and we also get to join in the groaning of all things suffering the consequences of our foolish war against him. Remember how David said that "the heavens declare the glory of God"? In the New Testament, Paul writes that they reveal something else as well:

> *The wrath of God is being revealed from heaven against all the godlessness and wickedness of people, who suppress the truth by their wickedness, since what may be known about God is plain to them, because God has made it plain to them. For since the creation of the world God's invisible qualities—his eternal power and divine nature—have been clearly seen, being understood from what has been made, so that people are without excuse. For although they knew God, they neither glorified him as God nor gave thanks to him, but their thinking became futile and their foolish hearts were darkened ... They exchanged the truth about God for a lie, and worshipped and served created things rather than the Creator—who is for ever praised. Amen.* (Romans 1:18-21, 25)

The heavens now declare two messages: one of glory, the other of wrath. Both messages are vital. First, we need to see the glory of the Creator who made us. We need to glimpse who he is so that we can respond to him properly. But now, because of humanity's rebellion against him, we also need a second message: we need to see what happens when we cut ourselves off from this glorious Creator. We need to see that no matter what we say, our lives still depend on our life-giver. We need a warning that the reinterpretive story we created that left him out of his own universe is a lie. A lie with devastating consequences. And to help us see this, God allows us a limited taste of those consequences while we live on Earth—and while we still have time to change course. He gave us the curse as a gift. Not a happy gift all wrapped up with a bow on it, but a hard, difficult, sad one—like the final last-hope surgical procedure that might cripple you and also might save your life. Except in this case, the lives he saves never end, while the crippling is only temporary. Even after the addition of pain and death to our world, the invitation that God originally built into creation—to know him and relate to him—still rings in our ears:

As surely as I live, declares the Sovereign Lord, I take no pleasure in the death of the wicked, but rather that they turn from their ways and live. Turn! Turn from your evil ways! Why will you die? (Ezekiel 33:11)

The curse is a wake-up call to shake humanity out of our lie so that we will turn back to the God who made us and find the life that only comes from him and never ends at all. The curse does not have to have the final word. Death does not have to have the final word. God knew that the fatal power of our lie could be broken—but he also knew that it wouldn't be easy. He knew that it would be so hard and costly that he would have to come and do it himself.

A Broken Curse

So he did. The Truth himself walked into our lie. God stepped out of glory and entered our groaning. The Creator became part of his creation. The writer stepped onto the stage. God's two languages came together in one physical body, one ultimate Rosetta Stone: "The Word became flesh and made his dwelling among us. We have seen his glory, the glory of the one and only Son, who came from the Father, full of grace and truth" (John 1:14).

And what did the living embodiment of truth come to do? He came not only to reveal God's truth to us but also to take on himself the consequences of our lie. Jesus became a human so that he could carry a cross on his own shoulders and die on it under the full weight of all our rejection, all our lies, all our rebellion and war and sin, and all the pain and suffering it brings. He did not stand aloof from our groaning; he entered into it. He took our sin, and it was so heavy that it buried him. Buried him like a seed—as he himself said: "Unless a grain of wheat falls to the ground and dies, it remains only a single seed. But if it dies, it produces many seeds" (12:24). Jesus could not stay dead. His life overthrew the grave, undid the power of the curse and brought unending life to every human who will repent, believe and accept the gift of his forgiveness and grace. Because of Jesus, life is still possible, even after death. The whole world, in all its glory and groaning, shouts to us to come back to our glorious Creator and warns us to stop misbelieving that we could ever live without him. Even after the curse, the invitation to know God remains. This is why God has not ended the world already; he leaves it broken because "he is patient with you, not wanting anyone to perish, but everyone to come to repentance" (2 Peter 3:9). He is waiting for us to respond to his communication. Waiting for us to accept his salvation. And all his creation waits too. Paul says:

I consider that our present sufferings are not worth comparing with the glory that will be revealed in us. For the creation waits in eager expectation for the children of God to be revealed. For the creation was subjected to frustration, not by its own choice, but by the will of the one who subjected it, in hope that the creation itself will be liberated from its bondage to decay and brought into the freedom and glory of the children of God. (Romans 8:18-21)

The goal of the curse is, ultimately, blessing. The goal of the groaning is glory for God's restored people, and God's restored creation. The end of the story of our world is not death and decay—the fading of autumn colour into eternal winter. The seed of life has already sprouted in the resurrection of Jesus Christ. The signs of spring are already beginning to show. The grip of winter is loosening, but we haven't made it to full summer yet. In the next verses, Paul writes that "the whole creation has been groaning as in the pains of childbirth right up to the present time. Not only so, but we ourselves, who have the firstfruits of the Spirit, groan inwardly as we wait eagerly for our adoption to sonship, the redemption of our bodies. For in this hope we were saved" (v 22-24).

We are not there yet. We feel our distance from the full realisation of this glorious hope constantly. We groan with creation, and creation groans with us. But although we experience groans of pain—they can be more than that. They can also be groans of expectation. The God who made this world knows how to remake it. The God who entered our groaning has the power to redeem it. The childbirth is painful, but it will end in new life.

CHAPTER 4

The Art of Interpretation

"The whole world is theology for us, because the heavens proclaim the glory of God."

Albert the Great

Once upon a time, you were born into a world of wonders. After that, everything was a discovery. It still is—though you might be too grown up to remember that. All you have to do is look closely at this world, and you'll be surprised. Guaranteed. And if you keep looking, you'll keep being surprised, so that you might end up living with your eyes perpetually popped wide, wondering what kind of fantastic fairy-tale universe God has put you in. The real world is actually more fantastic than any fairy tale. Fairy-tale fantasy always has a logical connection to realities we understand. A giant is a big human; a leprechaun is a little one. A unicorn is a horse with a horn, and that's easy to imagine because we already know about horses and horns. Our fantasy stories are remixed realities—they take the things we are familiar with and enhance or rearrange them to get our attention. The real world is the original mix, and it's far more creative than our stories.

Which is more fantastical: a horse with a horn or a horse with a six-foot-long neck, six-foot-long legs, and a bunch of giant freckles? Does it seem more likely for the real world to contain a large lizard that breathes fire or a small bug whose backside is a lightbulb? Does it seem more plausible that a pumpkin could turn into a carriage or that a caterpillar could melt itself into goo and rebuild itself into a flying work of art?

The truth really is stranger than fiction, and there's a good reason why: the creativity of our fantasies is only a subset of the creativity of God. Even our most imaginative stories are built on God's much more imaginative realities. Who would have dreamed up a mouse that flies in the dark using sonar and sleeps upside down? Who would have thought of filling the northern night sky with shining rivers of green and blue? God. That's who. The same God who wrote the recipe for glittering diamonds that can cut stone:

Ingredients: 1 pile of dead plants.

Leave covered indefinitely. Apply pressure.
When sparkling, cut and enjoy.

He didn't have to imagine the world this way. He didn't have to build in details like migrating birds and leaves that change colours. He didn't have to use the same "golden ratio" as his mathematical formula for everything from shells and hurricanes to pinecones and galaxies. But he did. Every detail is purposeful, written with God's hand, to say something to *you*.

Reading Reality

There's a moral to the story of reality. God's universe is not just endless creativity. It communicates truth and calls for a response—to glorify God, give him thanks and seek him. And just as the fantastic pictures on the pages of fairy-tale storybooks are interpreted for us by the words beside them, God has also given us words to accompany the illustrations of his reality. The art of interpreting creation is simply the process of understanding how the words of Scripture and the pictures of nature tell the same story. Look how Jesus interprets creation in Luke 12:

Therefore I tell you, do not worry about your life, what you will eat; or about your body, what you will wear. For life is more than food, and the body more than clothes. Consider the ravens: they do not sow or reap, they have no storeroom or barn; yet God feeds them. And how much more valuable you are than birds! Who of you by worrying can add a single hour to your life? Since you cannot do this very little thing, why do you worry about the rest? Consider how the wild flowers grow. They do not labour or spin. Yet I tell you, not even Solomon in all his splendour was dressed like one of these. If that is how God clothes the grass of the field, which is here today, and tomorrow is thrown into the fire, how much more will he clothe you—you of little faith! And do not set your heart on what you

*will eat or drink; do not worry about it. For the pagan
world runs after all such things, and your Father
knows that you need them. But seek his kingdom, and
these things will be given to you as well.*

(Luke 12:22-31)

Jesus tells us to consider the ravens and wild flowers
so that we will learn that the same God who cares
and provides for them also cares and provides for his
children. He is telling us directly that we can interpret
his creation and apply it to our lives. And he is showing
us how:

- First, Jesus encourages us to *discover* what God has
  made. He directs our thoughts to consider simple,
  easily observable truths about ravens and wild
  flowers that any child in a field can notice if only
  they pay attention. You don't need to be a scientist
  to hear the language of creation (although if you
  are, you might hear new and wonderful things).
  Mostly, you just need to pay attention.

- Next, Jesus demonstrates how to *interpret* what
  we discover in nature with the truth that God has
  revealed to us in his word. Why are the flowers
  so beautiful? Who clothed them this way? Who
  provides this food for the ravens? The Bible is clear:
  God is the fashion designer for flowers and the
  inventor of every raven-sustaining seed. You don't
  need to be a seasoned theologian to see how the
  languages of Scripture and nature speak the same
  message to us about the same God.

- Finally (and most importantly), Jesus encourages us to *respond*. He does not give us an abstract theological exercise. The reason why he tells us to consider the ravens and the wild flowers, and to apply our knowledge of God to our understanding of them, is because he wants us to respond to him. "Do not worry," he says. *Trust your Father and seek his kingdom first.* The end result of considering these plants and birds can be greater peace, less anxiety, and a clearer direction and security for our lives. All that from wild flowers and ravens!

What if we listened to everything this way? Could we also consider the mountains? The psalm writer does in Psalm 121:1. Could we consider the ants? Solomon tells us to in Proverbs 6:6-8. Could we consider the growth of crops? James does in James 5:7. All of creation communicates— it pours forth speech in a voice without words—and it is our privilege to discover, interpret and respond to what God says to us through it. Let's briefly consider each step.

DISCOVER

The first step towards learning the language of God's creation is simply to notice it—to pay attention to it and discover the truth about it. We arrive in this world knowing nothing, and a lifetime is not nearly enough time to discover all the wonders God has made. Every moment you are in God's world is an opportunity to listen to his voice in creation. I dare you to take even one step outside and really notice every part of creation around you. You'll never get to the end of it. Take a hike in the wilderness, and you'll be even more overwhelmed. Look more closely at the details, and you'll see that God's creation is more complex and creative than you'll be able to contain in familiar categories, and you can allow it to constantly expand your view of God. His whole universe is expanding, right now, isn't it? And yet we need powerful microscopes to detect the teeming detail in every millimetre. There is so much to discover!

INTERPRET

Every detail we discover in nature is meaningful. The hieroglyphics of God's creation are a language God meant for us to hear and understand and respond to— and he has given us the interpretive key in the Rosetta Stone of his word. When Jeremiah looked at creation, he said, "Ah, Sovereign LORD, you have made the heavens and the earth by your great power and outstretched arm. Nothing is too hard for you" (Jeremiah 32:17). He knew from Genesis 1 that God is the Creator, and he knew from simple observation that whoever can make this universe can do anything. He faithfully interpreted God's world by applying Scripture to it, and his interpretation helped him to know and trust God even more. These kinds of lessons are everywhere, which is why King Solomon was able to speak so many wise proverbs about creation:

> He spoke about plant life, from the cedar of Lebanon to the hyssop that grows out of walls. He also spoke about animals and birds, reptiles and fish.
>
> *(1 Kings 4:33)*

Here's one example: from Scripture, Solomon understood that our actions are really a reflection of our hearts (Deuteronomy 5:29 and 30:6). Then he looked at the world around him and saw a connection: "As water reflects the face, so one's life reflects the heart" (Proverbs 27:19). The reflective properties that God gave to still water helped Solomon understand what God says about our hearts more fully. But is this proverb the only interpretation possible for still water? No. Solomon's own father, King David, spoke of still water as a picture of God's provision (Psalm 23:2). It seems the old saying is true: still waters run deep—with meaning. The whole world runs deep. There is always more to discover and interpret. Some interpretations will be easy and straightforward, like Jeremiah's recognition of God's power. Others will be deeper and more complex, like Solomon's connection between water and hearts.

I am not King Solomon. You are not the prophet Jeremiah. So how confident can we be about our own interpretations of the world? Our understanding of the world, and of God's revealed word, is far from complete. Our feelings can mislead us, and our assumptions can blind us. We must approach this with humility. At the same time, we can have confidence in knowing that God wants to be known and has revealed himself to us. He has not left us alone; if we are his children, we have his promise that the Holy Spirit will guide us into all truth (John 16:13). He gives wisdom generously to those who ask him for it (James 1:5) and reveals himself so that we can know him (Deuteronomy 4:35). Creation is not a test. It is an invitation. If we don't understand some of it, we are free to ask the inventor and seek his help.

In all of this, we must recognise that we are only interpreting the meaning of God's creation, not writing it. The meaning is already there, and our task is to understand it—not reinvent it for our own purposes. When Job's friends visited him in his suffering, they made long speeches that eloquently interpreted many aspects of God's creation and Job's situation in the light of their own personal favourite truth about God: that he justly judges those who do wrong. In doing so, they completely ignored other important truths about God's character, and the result was that they misinterpreted Job's situation, the meaning of creation, and ultimately God himself. In the end, God told them, "You have not spoken the truth about me" (Job 42:7). Let this not be said of us.

In our search for the truth, we cannot pick and choose which of God's words are important, invent our own view of what he is like, or reinterpret the message of his creation to suit our own sensibilities. We intentionally seek out the whole truth, even when it makes us uncomfortable. By all means, we ought to enjoy the familiar places we love—the verses we love in Scripture, and the gardens and woods and beaches we love in creation. But God also speaks to us through the wastelands, the crows, and the nettles. Are you listening to *them*? Are you paying attention to the sections of Scripture that stretch your concept of God and don't fit well into your preconceived boxes? If we're not careful, we'll miss a lot of what God is saying to us, simply because we're not sure we'll like what it means. But the goal is not to come up with the meaning we like best. It is to hear what God is actually saying to us about what is actually true. Remember, "the truth will set you free" (John 8:32). But the goal of hearing what God is saying to us is not merely to understand him. It is to respond to him.

RESPOND

The final step in reading reality is the most important. In chapter 2, we saw that David's primary concern as he heard God's voice in both creation and Scripture was to *respond* correctly: "May these words of my mouth and this meditation of my heart be pleasing in your sight, LORD, my Rock and my Redeemer" (Psalm 19:14). This final step in learning creation's language is the most important by far—the step that everything else is meant to lead us to. God did not give us his glorious creation as a curiosity to keep us occupied. He did not wind up a useful machine and leave us alone with it. He gave us his creation as a revelation; he made himself known and invites us to know him. Its beauty is a reflection of his own glory; its awe-inspiring power and wisdom and design is his work, meant to lift our eyes and draw our hearts to awe and worship, trust and love, and a never-ending desire to know and enjoy the Creator behind every wonder of creation. Even the groaning of creation can stir our hearts to hope for his salvation and eternal restoration in Christ. A true understanding of creation and a faithful interpretation of its meaning should always lead us towards knowing, loving, worshipping and following the God who spoke it into existence. That's the whole point.

Are you paying attention to God's voice in his creation? He is speaking to you through it constantly. He has given you everything you need to interpret it in his word. Even now—you can take a walk or gaze out of the window or look down and examine the artistry of your own hands. God's voice is calling you. He is inviting you to know him. Are you responding to him?

There is much more that we could say about these things, but rather than simply talking about them, let's put them into practice. For the rest of this book, we'll use the days of creation in Genesis 1 as a framework to discover, interpret and respond to the voice of God in his many varied wonders.

PART II

To Hear and Respond

CHAPTER 5

Let There
Be Light

*"Darkness cannot drive out darkness;
only light can do that."*

Martin Luther King, Jr.

It was the middle of night, in the middle of nowhere. Eight teenage boys were suspended in hammocks beside each other, in a shelter made of logs lashed together with twine and a tarp for a roof. There were tripod towers at the corners and thick crossbeams but the sides of the shelter were open, which may have been why we woke so quickly when the scuffling started outside. It was noisy—and close. "What's *that?*" my friend Daniel whispered, through clenched teeth, as I reached for my Maglite torch with its four C batteries in the handle and the brightest beam a Boy Scout could afford. In a pinch, I figured that light was heavy enough to serve as a weapon against whatever was out there making those noises. Teenage boys think this way.

There was no need. Ben was already outside shouting, "There's a raccoon the size of New York, and he's in our supplies!" I ducked my head under the edge of the shelter just in time to see the backside of our burglar as he scurried away. There were lights pointing everywhere now and excited voices assessing the situation. He hadn't taken much, thankfully. We strung up the rest of our supplies off the ground and went back to bed. In the morning, the Alabama sun was so bright that it hurt my eyes even through the roof-tarp, and our midnight visitor might as well have been in New York because we never saw him again.

Discovering Light

In the beginning God created the heavens and the earth. Now the earth was formless and empty, darkness was over the surface of the deep, and the Spirit of God was hovering over the waters. And God said, "Let there be light," and there was light. God saw that the light was good, and he separated the light from the darkness. God called the light "day", and the darkness he called "night". And there was evening, and there was morning—the first day. (Genesis 1:1-5)

On the first day of creation, God turned the lights on. I understand that because turning the lights on is usually my first priority too. Whether it's in a shelter in the woods or the safety of home, I like to see what's going on and where I'm going. Raccoons scavenge at night because their eyes have a structure called a tapetum lucid that helps them see with minimal light—and also because they are thieves and darkness is an advantage when you're robbing people blind; but I have neither these advantages nor these motivations. What I do have is light, and I make sure to always have a source of it close by.

What we call "light" is the visible portion of a wide spectrum of electromagnetic radiation—a spectrum that also includes radio waves, X-rays and microwaves. If our eyes were equipped to detect more of this spectrum, we could see our voices broadcasting out of our phones and the colours of the music on the radio. This sounds fascinating, but I'm sure it would be overwhelming to see all of these frequencies all the time, so I'm happy to focus on the range God equipped me for. It's wonder enough, yet I'm so used to it that I hardly appreciate it. Usually, I only think about the things light shows me, like the chair, the tree, or the smiling face. But I wouldn't see any of those things without the light revealing them to me. To see, I depend on a steady stream of light-photons pouring into my eyes, which are specially equipped to interpret the waving frequencies of those photons into the colours and shapes of reality. How light can be a physical particle and a wave at the same time is complicated. God is an artist who paints with physics. And he literally gave us the eyes to see it.

Interpreting Light

Jesus said, "Your eye is the lamp of your body. When your eyes are healthy, your whole body also is full of light. But when they are unhealthy, your body also is full of darkness. See to it, then, that the light within you is not darkness. Therefore, if your whole body is full of light, and no part of it dark, it will be just as full of light as when a lamp shines its light on you" (Luke 11:34-36).

It may sound obvious, but Jesus is reminding us that the light we see comes from outside of us. We don't create it; we receive it. And he's not just talking about physical light because his application is to "see to it, then, that the light within you is not darkness" (v 35). So the hieroglyphics of physical light and darkness must be pointing to deeper realities—but we already knew that. Don't people love to talk about finding the "light within"? We're told we must look inside ourselves, find the light, and shine it out to the world around us. This is compelling as a metaphor, but it certainly does not work literally. You can test that: go ahead and roll your eyes up into your head and look for light. Look inside yourself for as long as you like. I'll wait.

God did give some parts of his creation the ability to produce light. Stars most of all, but also glow-worms, lanternfish, bioluminescent plankton, molten rock and clouds dramatically throwing out electrical charges. If he wanted us to have a literal light within us, he could have easily included one in his design. I can imagine plenty of situations where that feature would be useful, including (but not limited to) dealing with raccoons. Never mind, it's not there. Which means that the physical reality we need to interpret is not actually our inner light. It's our inner darkness. What is God saying to us by making us rely on light as an external rather than an internal reality?

"See to it, then, that the light within you is not darkness." To have light, you must open your eyes. You must receive what is given from another source. That's true for physical light, and it's true for the light of knowledge, hope and truth as well. If you only look inside yourself for these realities, you'll find that the "light within you" is darkness. This is why we have an education system, and why how-to videos and social-media advisors are so popular. But if you're only looking to other people for light, remember that they can't create it either. Is the light they're pointing you to *really* light or only another shade of darkness? How will you know the difference? Where is a reliable light source? David wrote in Psalm 19 that "the commands of the LORD are radiant, giving light to the eyes" (v 8). Again, in another psalm he says, "The unfolding of your words gives light; it gives understanding to the simple" (119:130). The same God who reveals the world with physical light also reveals his truth through the words of Scripture. And he went further: after speaking to us in both of those languages, he came to Earth himself and spoke to us in person—both in words and in actions like healing the blind. He said, "I am the light of the world. Whoever follows me will never walk in darkness, but will have the light of life" (John 8:12). Jesus is the Creator behind our physical light, and the ultimate Word behind the words of Scripture. When he came to Earth, he did not come as one more light among many—he came as the source of all true light.

Responding to Light

Jesus reveals more to us than the light of the sun ever could, but we must open our eyes and receive his revelation. He said we must come "into the light" (John 3:21). Just come. Is it that easy? Remember, the light of Christ is pure and bright. In heaven, God "lives in unapproachable light" (1 Timothy 6:16). This is not the cosy light of a small, susurrating flame. It's more like a search light that reveals every shadow—every dark, dirty corner of our hearts. The hidden rooms we locked and left to gather dust. The secrets we covered and tried to forget. The shame. Do we really want the light to shine on us? Jesus said, "This is the verdict: light has come into the world, but people loved darkness instead of light because their deeds were evil. Everyone who does evil hates the light, and will not come into the light for fear that their deeds will be exposed. But whoever lives by the truth comes into the light, so that it may be seen plainly that what they have done has been done in the sight of God" (John 3:19-21).

Our fear of coming into God's light is that it will expose us—which is true. That's what light does. But remember, the light of his truth will shine on us anyway. His eyes are better than ours. Better than raccoon eyes. They see everything that is done in the darkness (Psalm 139:11-12). Jesus said, "There is nothing hidden that will not be disclosed, and nothing concealed that will not be known or brought out into the open" (Luke 8:17). There's no point in hiding what God already knows. And there's no need to; Jesus came to earth to pay the price for our sin and shame on the cross—all of it—if we'll only trust him and come into his light. So, unlock the dusty rooms. Throw open the doors. Tear down the curtains. The light Jesus came to shine on you is not the searchlight of justice (unless you insist on hiding in the darkness). The light he came to bring you is "the light of *life*" (John 8:12).

Imagine a sick, drooping houseplant shying away from the light because it is ashamed of how pale its stem is, how limp its leaves are. It never happens. Why? Because houseplants are not as proud as we are. They do not pretend that they can live off their own light. Even without legs, they grow and strain and reach for the sun. They do not conceal their sickness or hide their needs. They simply receive. And in the light, they live. In the light, they heal. They thrive and grow.

God has not left us in darkness. He did not make us to create our own light, but he did equip us to receive light from him. So, open your eyes. Come into the light and let it expose you and heal you. Let his truth and his words be the lamp that guides your feet and the light that directs your path (Psalm 119:105). When you do this, you also begin to reflect his light. Jesus didn't only say, "I am the light of the world"; he also said, "You are the light of the world ... Let your light shine before others, that they may see your good deeds and glorify your Father in heaven" (Matthew 5:14, 16). Why would people glorify God for the good deeds of his people? Because their good is a reflection of his. He is the sun; we are the moon. If we shine at all, we shine with a brightness and glory received from another source. Did God leave night in his creation to help us understand this? As you see the silver moonbeams breaking through the darkness, or the sunlight falling on the leaves that lean in to receive it, or the warm glow of a fire dancing in the hearth, let the photons pouring into your eyes also pour their meaning into your mind: the Light of the world is speaking with you.

CHAPTER 6

A Never-Ending Newsfeed

"The best remedy for those who are frightened, lonely or unhappy is to go outside, somewhere they can be alone, alone with the sky, nature and God."

Anne Frank

Newsfeeds never end. That's the genius of social media—there's always something more, something different to see, if you keep looking. I refresh my feeds to stay up to date on the latest news of the world and the people I know in it, but I have to admit that some of my favourite content is pictures of this world we live in. I like it when a friend captures a great sunset over the ocean and shares it with me. You know what I mean— the #nofilter kind. The kind with oranges and reds in it that make the words "orange" and "red" feel like post-it notes slapped on a Van Gogh.

Some of my friends are great photographers. Still, I've never seen a picture that was anything more than a tantalising taste of a real experience. One of the most impressive sunrises I've ever seen happened over Myrtle Beach, South Carolina. I'd rather take you there than show you my photo though. When you actually see the sky light up over the ocean while the waves are crashing at your feet and you feel the salt on your skin, then, yes, of course you'll want to pull out your phone and capture that moment as well, but you'll never capture the whole thing any more than a photograph of your mother's smile or a video of her laugh can capture the full experience of spending time in her company. Our pictures will never be as real as the realities they picture.

On the second day of creation, "God said, 'Let there be a vault between the waters to separate water from water.' So God made the vault and separated the water under the vault from the water above it. And it was so. God called the vault 'sky'. And there was evening, and there was morning—the second day" (Genesis 1:6-8). God separated the sky from the water, and in doing this, he created one of his most famous artistic canvases.

Discovering Sky

We are breathing creatures. Life depends on air. We are drinking creatures too. Life depends on water. So when God separated the waters from the sky, he still connected them through an intricate cycle: salty depths that evaporate into fluffy, white freshwater-storehouse blimps floating above our heads—with built-in sprinkler systems equipped to quench the thirst of all living things. Ever since I was a child, I have wondered how God made water fly. How does *that* work?

It works brilliantly. It provides exactly what we need to live, both the air to breathe and the fresh water to drink. But the system is not just pure efficiency. When God invented the sky, he made it into a massive expanse—an unframeable canvas. And ever since, he has been painting on that canvas constantly. Most days, in most places, he paints it with shades of blue—but even then, he constantly remixes those blues throughout the day. Sometimes he transforms it by painting bright colours all over the sky with sunrises or auroras. There are other times when he leaves the world under a grey blanket, draining away all of the colours while he gathers them together and then hangs them out to dry as a rainbow. This sign is his promise that whatever storms may come, they will not destroy the world again as they did when Noah and his family and the animals needed a boat to survive God's judgment on sinful humanity (Genesis 9:12-17).

We need that promise because the storms do come. Where I grew up in Alabama, we had air-raid sirens that went off several times a year—but the threat was not from enemy airplanes; it was from clouds. Those friendly, fluffy storehouse blimps with their life-giving sprinklers sometimes grow into gigantic enemy airships: dirigibles of death, slinging hail and electric fire and—worst of all—tornadoes. Cows flew. Houses too. The waters heaved. God's canvas above us can be beautiful in the extreme—or deadly. Either way, it is overwhelming.

Interpreting Sky

God once spoke to a man directly out of a whirlwind. In chapter 38 of the book of Job, after Job's many questions, God's answer began by drawing attention to his creation:

Where were you when I laid the earth's foundation?
  Tell me, if you understand.
Who marked off its dimensions? Surely you know!
  Who stretched a measuring line across it?   *(v 4-5)*

Who shut up the sea behind doors
  when it burst forth from the womb,
when I made the clouds its garment
  and wrapped it in thick darkness … ?   *(v 8-9)*

Have you ever given orders to the morning,
  or shown the dawn its place … ?   *(v 12)*

Have you entered the storehouses of the snow
  or seen the storehouses of the hail … ?   *(v 22)*

Can you raise your voice to the clouds
  and cover yourself with a flood of water?
Do you send the lightning bolts on their way?
  Do they report to you, "Here we are"?   *(v 34-35)*

There's more. But you get the point—the power and beauty of God's sky is supposed to overwhelm us. It is supposed to remind us of who we are, and who God is. In that sense, the sky is God's never-ending newsfeed, constantly updating, always refreshing with new content, new information, new revelation about the one who spoke it into existence:

The heavens declare the glory of God;
  the skies proclaim the work of his hands
Day after day they pour forth speech;
  night after night they reveal knowledge.
                                        (Psalm 19:1-2)

God doesn't have to speak to us directly out of the whirlwind as he did with Job. He is already speaking to us through the whirlwind itself. It preaches to us of God's glory, strength, holiness and authority (Psalm 29). It reminds us of the trouble we both face and cause, in a world broken by humanity's sinful rebellion against God:

You have been a refuge for the poor,
  a refuge for the needy in their distress,
a shelter from the storm
  and a shade from the heat.
For the breath of the ruthless
  is like a storm driving against a wall   *(Isaiah 25:4)*

But the storms caused by sinful people are no match for the storm of God's judgment against them, when it falls:

See, the storm of the Lord
  will burst out in wrath,
a whirlwind swirling down
  on the heads of the wicked.   *(Jeremiah 23:19)*

There are no storms in heaven. No sin. No judgment. No cursed creation. But until then, we need displays of God's power, authority and righteous wrath against sin. We're prone to forget. We're prone to think that it's perfectly fine for us to carry on acting as if we are the real gods who make the world for ourselves. So we *need* to be overwhelmed. We need a wake-up call to make us realise that the world is not right, and we are not right, and we have to make our peace with the true God of creation. The storms are real, and the warning they bring is real and serious—but so is the rainbow that follows and the promise of God's gift of mercy and grace to those who put their trust in him. His goal is not to destroy us; it is to bring us to himself—or why would he make the storms so infrequent and our normal experience of the sky a series of overwhelming beauties? We need more than displays of God's power; we need displays of God's grace. And we have them. Whatever we have done, we still have air. We still have sunsets. The same God who warns us from above also provides for us out of the same sky, whether we deserve it or not. Jesus said:

> *He causes his sun to rise on the evil and the good,*
> *and sends rain on the righteous and the unrighteous.*
> *(Matthew 5:45)*

This is good rain—the kind we need to quench our thirst and grow our food. So the same sky that speaks of God's justice also declares his love—even for his enemies. The expanse that speaks of his power and authority also speaks of his joyful generosity. It makes us feel small and powerless, and at the same time, it draws us in to celebrate the beauty and care of our Creator:

> *The whole earth is filled with awe at your wonders;*
> *where morning dawns, where evening fades, you call*
> *forth songs of joy.*   *(Psalm 65:8)*

Responding to Sky

It is good for us to remember, like David, Jeremiah, Isaiah and Job, that God's newsfeeds overrule ours. The next time you're discouraged and down from the never-ending stream of bad news and depressing events online, here's something to try: take a break from refreshing your screen and be refreshed instead by a display of God's majesty in his natural newsfeed. Look up at the sky. Inhale the power and authority of a God who can command water to separate above and below to give us breathing space. Soak in the wisdom of clouds. When they, in turn, soak you with their driving rain and wild winds, remember the one who stilled them with his command, and who stilled God's judgment with his sacrifice. See his sky and be overwhelmed by a world outside of your normal walls and ceilings—a world that is too much for you. You are not the centre of it, and you can't control it, but you can enjoy it and enjoy its Creator.

Read the news of God's power, and do not fear the powers of earth. Read the news of his care, and cast your cares on him (1 Peter 5:7). Read the colours of his delight, and sing for joy and wonder (Psalm 65:8). Just as our newsfeeds point us to the people and realities beyond the posts and pictures themselves, God's sky points us beyond itself to the Author of reality. As superior as God's natural newsfeed is to our flat, digital chaos, it is still only a glimpse—albeit a massive, overwhelming glimpse—of the God who is far, far greater and more glorious than the most beautiful aurora show or terrifying typhoon. As Job put it:

He spreads out the northern skies over empty space;
he suspends the earth over nothing.
He wraps up the waters in his clouds,
yet the clouds do not burst under their weight.
He covers the face of the full moon,
spreading his clouds over it.
He marks out the horizon on the face of the waters
for a boundary between light and darkness.
The pillars of the heavens quake,
aghast at his rebuke.
By his power he churned up the sea ...
By his breath the skies became fair ...
And these are but the outer fringe of his works;
how faint the whisper we hear of him!
Who then can understand the thunder of his power?
(Job 26:7-14)

The language of the sky overwhelms us because it speaks to us of a God who is overwhelming. Every aspect of God is beyond us—his power, his authority, his justice, his beauty, his creativity, his love; all are greater than we can comprehend. Even the glimpses we see, the whispers we hear of him in the expanse of his sky, can be too much for us. And that's okay. Look up. God's newsfeed never ends, and it's good to be overwhelmed.

CHAPTER 7

The Chaos Container

"There is one knows not what sweet mystery about this sea, whose gently awful stirrings seem to speak of some hidden soul beneath."

Herman Melville, in *Moby Dick*

With our wetsuits on, my children and I were able to walk confidently into the cold water. It was the height of summer, but the water in the Celtic Sea is never warm. A couple of millimetres of neoprene protection makes it much more enjoyable. The waves looked good that day, and we walked out to where they were breaking so that we could catch some. My son was beside me, but as the water drove us back towards the beach, our bodyboards collided, and we laughed as my daughter flew past us on a fast one. We cheered her on, picked up our boards, and went again. And again. And again.

My legs were tired, but the waves were never tired. They kept hitting me with the same power: pushing and pulling and pushing again. Sometimes they came up unexpectedly and broke on top of me, taking my breath away with cold and surprise—but I didn't mind. Nearby I saw the waves breaking on the rocks at the base of a cliff, shattering into a thousand waterfalls and running down fast so they could hit the rocks again. And again. And again.

There is immense power in the water. That's why the lifeguard set the swimming zone well away from the rocks. That's why he used a loudspeaker to warn us that there was a strong riptide that day, so we'd better not go far. We could play in the water and have a great time—just as long as we respected its power. When the cold waves slapped us in the face again and again, we remembered that we were small and mortal and that the waves were stronger than we were. And we laughed.

Discovering the Sea

On the third day, "God said, 'Let the water under the sky be gathered to one place, and let dry ground appear.' And it was so. God called the dry ground 'land', and the gathered waters he called 'seas'. And God saw that it was good" (Genesis 1:9-10). After separating light from darkness and sky from water, God gathered those waters together and separated them from the land. He called them "seas", and they were not only good—they were big. Oceans cover more than 70 percent of the surface of our planet and hold more than 350 quintillion gallons of water. They hide mountain ranges beneath their waves, and their deepest point is almost seven miles below the surface. That's a lot of water. Is blue God's favourite colour?

As humans, our primary concerns with this water are usually to catch food from it, play around its edges, and cross it in boats with railings because nobody wants to go overboard. You can't stand in the water, and you can't swim for ever. Sharks exist. That's why our maps of the world usually focus on the land. Even our imaginary maps for places like Middle-earth and Narnia are land maps, mostly. If you were drawing the map of a new planet, would you cover most of it with unpredictable, dangerously powerful water? That's what God did. At first glance, this may seem like a strange, excessive choice. It may look like a wasteful use of the earth's limited space. Is it?

Did you know that the earth's oceans produce more than half of the oxygen our lives depend on? This is mostly the work of microscopic phytoplankton, which also absorbs CO_2. Did you know that your ability to breathe was so dependent on plants you can't see? And that's only the beginning. The ocean also produces clouds as its water evaporates in the sun, and helps produce the air currents that drive those clouds inland, where they drop fresh, life-giving water on our heads. On our crops. On our rivers, which cut through the land like irrigation channels, filled with never-ending provision (Ecclesiastes 1:7; Psalm 1:3). As the clouds form, the oceans also absorb the heat of the sun and store it, like massive solar panels. Then, through their continuous currents, they redistribute this warmth to the colder areas of Earth and bring moderating coolness to the warmer ones. Without the oceans, Earth's land would be dry, its temperatures would be extreme, and its air would be toxic. The lines on God's map are not wasteful.

Still, the sea is a paradox. We need it to live, but its power can kill us. It creates life-giving rainclouds and spawns death-wielding hurricanes. We can pull food from it or be pulled away by its overpowering force. Its never-ending waves can calm our minds or terrify them. They can relax our bodies like a cradle or toss them as if they're a toy. How do we interpret such an unpredictable, uncontrollable, awe-inspiring, beautiful and dangerous reality?

Interpreting the Sea

Throughout the Bible, the sea is recognised as a chaotic, unstable and unpredictable force. If you've ever been out of your depth in the ocean, you'll understand why. The danger can hit hard and fast. In fact, the sea is the very first image of chaos and disorder ever given, right at the very beginning, before the days of creation have started. In Genesis 1:2, when the earth was still "formless and empty", it was covered with water. Uninhabitable and inhospitable. To make the earth our home, God had to bring the land up out of the sea and set boundaries to contain the force of its waters (Jeremiah 5:22). Inside those boundaries, the sea remains. And its power is often seen in Scripture as a picture—a hieroglyph of all the forces of chaos and destruction. Including people. Isaiah 17:12 says:

Woe to the many nations that rage—
  they rage like the raging sea!
Woe to the peoples who roar—
  they roar like the roaring of great waters!

When people combine their power together as nations, they can become a significant force. Because of our sin, however, this force is often chaotic and unpredictable, and used for destructive purposes. The nations churn and heave and crash against each other like the tossing sea, billowing up the foam of threats and curses against the God who made them, as well. Instead of using our power as humans to cultivate and care for God's good gifts, we regularly use our strength to tear his world and each other apart, for the sake of our own selfish ends. But as powerful as the sea is, and as powerful as people can be, no force of nature or human might can overpower the Creator. Isaiah 17:13 continues:

Although the peoples roar like the roar
  of surging waters,
    when he rebukes them they flee far away,
driven before the wind like chaff on the hills,
  like tumble-weed before a gale.

The sea may be chaotic, but it is contained. Its boundary lines are drawn. The Creator of the oceans is not intimidated by their power or size. He "measure[s] the waters in the hollow of his hand" (40:12)—all 350 quintillion gallons. And the raging nations? They are nothing but a "drop in a bucket" (v 15).

You rule over the surging sea;
when its waves mount up, you still them.

(Psalm 89:9)

When John describes heaven, he speaks of calm waters (Revelation 4:6), a life-giving river (22:1), and an end to the chaos of the oceans (21:1). But we don't live there yet. We live in a creation still waiting and groaning for restoration. And as we wait, we see God allowing waves, and nations and troubles and disasters, to surge for a season. That does not mean he has lost control over them. Far from it. In fact, he turns the contained chaos of the oceans into provision for us—sustaining life with oxygen, rain and warmth. And in a similar way, he also provides good for his children through the contained chaos of humanity.

Think about it: the worst act of human rebellion ever conceived or carried out was the deliberate killing of the Son of God himself. And Jesus allowed our tsunami of sin to take his life. He knew that the final result would not be his destruction; it would be the destruction of the tsunami. It would be the beginning of our restoration, and of all creation with us. If God can turn the greatest act of evil in all history into the greatest imaginable result, can he not also keep his promise that in "all things God works for the good of those who love him" (Romans 8:28)? All things? Yes. Even the chaos and trouble of this world are used by God to refine our faith like gold (1 Peter 1:6-7). To perfect our character (James 1:2-4) and correct us when we wander (Hebrews 12:5-10). He uses them to achieve for us "an eternal glory that far outweighs" our "light and momentary troubles" (2 Corinthians 4:17). The chaos may confuse us, and the trouble may be far beyond our control, but it is not beyond his. He will force all things to do his children good, in the end. And on the way to that good, he also promised his people, "When you pass through the waters, I will be with you" (Isaiah 43:2).

Responding to the Sea

When the Creator of the oceans became a man, he walked on the waves (Matthew 14:22-33). This was not only a powerful act but it was a symbolic one: the Prince of Peace was stepping on the hieroglyph of chaos. He also commanded the waves to be still, and they had to obey (Mark 4:35-41). Then he turned to his trembling disciples and said, "Why are you so afraid? Do you still have no faith?" (v 40). Yes, the world is still groaning under the weight of the curse until it is fully restored. But although the chaotic forces of nature and the destructive power of evil may look overpowering from our perspective, we need not face them alone. The Lord who commanded the waves and taught his disciples to trust him through the storm is still trustworthy. The God who made the sea is strong enough to contain it. The Saviour who defeated death by dying can bring glory and good out of any trouble. Why are you so afraid?

God is our refuge and strength,
an ever-present help in trouble.
Therefore we will not fear, though the earth give way
and the mountains fall into the heart of the sea,

though its waters roar and foam
and the mountains quake with their surging.

There is a river whose streams make glad
the city of God,
the holy place where the Most High dwells.
God is within her, she will not fall;
God will help her at break of day.
Nations are in uproar, kingdoms fall;
he lifts his voice, the earth melts ...

He says, "Be still, and know that I am God;
I will be exalted among the nations,
I will be exalted in the earth."

The LORD Almighty is with us;
the God of Jacob is our fortress.

(Psalm 46:1-6, 10-11)

CHAPTER 8

The Clay and
the Potter

*"Until we understand what the land is, we are at
odds with everything we touch."*

Wendell Berry

My children and I peeled ourselves out of our wetsuits and sat down in the sand. Our bodies were tired from being pushed against the constant power of the ocean, but our hearts were happy. We revived ourselves by soaking in the warmth of the sun, the mysteries of Agatha Christie, and the calming sound of the contained sea. After a while, someone picked up a shovel.

When our family goes on holiday, we're laid back about pretty much everything. Except sandcastles. Over the last several years, we've developed a holiday tradition of building the biggest and best sandcastle we can manage. Every holiday, they get bigger. Every holiday, they get better, as we discover new techniques and develop our abilities. A few years ago, we learned the advantage of building on rock outcroppings, for protection and beauty. Then we learned how to straighten the walls with the edge of a shovel and dig under them to create arched doorways. We learned the best kinds of sand to build with and the best kinds of rocks and shells to decorate with. We learned to make towers with pointed roofs, churches with sea-glass windows, and walled seaweed gardens. We're well aware that our creations can't last, but why did God make grains of sand stick together so well, if not for this? I know that's simplistic, but I don't believe it's wrong. I believe our Father in heaven delights in the laughter of his children when they're playing in his sandpit. I believe he knew exactly what he was doing when he invented beaches.

On the third day, "God said, 'Let the water under the sky be gathered to one place, and let dry ground appear.' And it was so. God called the dry ground 'land', and the gathered waters he called 'seas'. And God saw that it was good" (Genesis 1:9-10).

Discovering Land

In the far, far away galaxy of *Star Wars,* each planet has its own unique biome: a desert world, an ice world, or a moon-forest full of alien teddy bears. Here on Earth, we have them all (including bears). Still, looking closely at the ground God made for us might seem like a bit of a distraction—like looking at the boards of the Globe Theatre instead of watching *King Lear.* But look at the boards! When God designs a set, he doesn't cut corners. He could have made just a few basics—one type of rock, one kind of soil, and maybe some sand scattered here and there for good measure. That would surely have done the job and given him a sufficient foundation to move on to the more interesting bits. But instead, he set the stage of Earth with complex beauty, wide variety and huge potential. There are cliffs towering over the waves, and sandy beaches welcoming them. There are wide deserts and frozen tundras and plateaus cracked with canyons, and don't forget the mountains—some of them breathe fire and sit on treasure stores of gold and precious jewels in their deep, dark caverns. No, there's nothing bland about land.

God set this stage, and he meant for us to pay attention to his work, not just walk around on it. He made it beautiful and interesting and dramatic—he filled it with hidden treasures, and he did all of this on purpose. The cliffs communicate. The endless prairies speak an endless message. The mountains rise above the landscape like monumental steeples, directing our eyes upward (Psalm 121:1-2). And what about those treasure hoards underneath? God knew exactly what he was doing when he buried them.

Land is our home. It is the setting for all terrestrial life, the ground for every garden, the rock for every foundation, the soil for every tree. Its many various forms provide exactly what is needed to sustain the many various kinds of life God filled it with—including us. It is a sculpture more exquisite and detailed than any masterpiece in a museum, but it has no glass and no security system to keep us from touching it. In fact, the artist encourages us to touch it. "The LORD God took the man and put him in the Garden of Eden to work it and take care of it" (Genesis 2:15).

Interpreting Land

What do you think of when you hear the word "paradise"? Does it cast your mind back to an idyllic garden, untouched by human civilisation? It's a popular image, and a powerful one. We see the beauty of the world around us and also how many of our developments detract from it. Car parks cover the grass, power lines cut the sky, and even our earth-friendly wind turbines aren't friendly to the birds and bats who run into their blades. Wouldn't it be better for Earth if humanity left it alone and quit touching everything so much?

The answer of Scripture is "No". The path to paradise in the Bible is not a return to the earth's natural, wild, uncultivated beginnings. The garden God gave Adam and Eve was an idyllic foundation to work from, certainly, but it was never intended to be the finished product. God did not tell Adam and Eve to leave his garden alone because they would spoil it by interfering—he told them to work it and keep it. He told them to "be fruitful and increase in number; fill the earth and subdue it" (Genesis 1:28). He gave humanity a world bursting with potential, and he put us here on purpose to develop it. In doing so, he intended for us to reflect the image of the one who made us (v 27). He is the Potter, but he gave us clay to work with as well. He is the Artist who provided us with our own canvas and colours. He is the Architect who handed us our own building blocks. He set this stage for us and filled it with all the props and resources we need to reflect his character and proclaim his goodness and praise.

There are times—flashes of brilliance—when humanity does this well, but overall we've failed. There's no sense in denying it. Instead of working with our Creator and using his resources to develop a home that reflects his righteousness, justice, creativity and care, we have worked against him and misused his many good gifts to promote our own pride and feed our own greed. Instead of protecting creation from harm, we have often harmed it ourselves and harnessed its potential to harm each other—the very people God specifically told us to reflect his love to.

Still, God's purposes for his creation haven't changed. The story of history is not yet finished, and the ending is glorious. In the book of Revelation, John describes a restored Earth, with plenty of the natural elements of Eden like rivers and trees—and more besides; there will also be a holy city, filled with gold and jewels and light, established as a home where all God's children can live with him for ever (Revelation 21 – 22). Did you catch that? The ultimate fulfilment of paradise is not a return to an untouched garden. Paradise is a garden city, growing in harmony with the world around it and beautified with the mined and polished treasures of earth.

If it's hard to imagine how a city could grow *with* nature instead of *against* it; that's probably because of how badly we've failed at the task God gave us. Can you imagine if the creative energy of humanity were fully aligned with the creative purposes of God? That would be paradise.

Responding to Land

Looking around the world today, it may seem that this kind of paradise is a long way off. So many of humanity's interactions with the land God gave us are destructive—to the land and, ultimately, to ourselves. Even when our intentions and goals are good, our work with the land is painful and difficult as a result of the curse of sin (Genesis 3:17-19). There are thorns to deal with now, and decay, entropy and frustration. Even so, the land God gave us is still bursting with potential for good, and it is still the privilege and responsibility of humanity to reflect the image of our Creator by creatively working and developing the raw materials he made us for his purposes. Just because many people are still working against God and exploiting his natural gifts for their own ends doesn't mean we have to keep doing that ourselves.

We can pursue a different course and return to our original task of working and keeping. We can be like the ancient Israelites Bezalel and Oholiab, whom God commissioned to build a tabernacle of praise, filling them "with wisdom, with understanding, with knowledge and with all kinds of skills—to make artistic designs for work in gold, silver and bronze, to cut and set stones, to work in wood and to engage in all kinds of artistic crafts" (Exodus 35:31-33). Does the work of our hands bring praise to our Maker? Does our use of his materials reflect his purposes? It's not an accident that rocks are strong enough to build homes that provide shelter and security. It's not an accident that copper conducts electricity to light those homes at night, or that sand can be made into windows that let the sun shine through during the day. The question is not whether we should use the resources God gave us. The question is: what are we using them for, and how?

God meant for us to grow food from the land and to mine its resources. But he also meant for us to care for it and protect it. He told his people they should not needlessly cut trees (Deuteronomy 20:19). He also told them to let their farmland rest at regular intervals (Exodus 23:10-11). They were to respect the land and care for it as a gift from God, even as it provided for their needs. I wonder what it would look like today if we approached the land with the same attitude? It would certainly look different from much of what we see around us. Our choice as we engage with the land is not a simple binary one between saving it from ourselves or exploiting it for ourselves. The problem with both of these options is the exclusive focus on ourselves and our world. The missing ingredient in both is God—the Creator of both us and our world. When we recognise whose world this is, our work in it can begin to take its proper shape. When we recognise his character, we'll begin to understand the purposes behind his charge to protect what he made for us.

If you want to follow God's commands and are aiming your efforts at his priorities, then, by all means, you can use the resources he gave you to do that well. Jesus himself was a carpenter. So make the instruments, and play them (Psalm 150). Build the buildings, and make the doors wide for hospitality. Create the art, and let it reflect the greatest Artist. Mould the pottery, and use it for the greatest Potter. Wire the electronics. Mix the medicines. Plant the crops. And as you make use of these gifts of his provision, remember your responsibility towards the land he gave us, as well. We are the workers and keepers, the cultivators and guardians of God's world. As we interact with his gift of land, we should always seek to do so in ways that lead to thriving—not only for ourselves but for all of God's creation. He gave you your fingers, and he never meant for you to leave his world untouched.

CHAPTER 9

The Seeds of Life

"Earth's crammed with heaven,
And every common bush afire with God,
But only he who sees takes off his shoes;
The rest sit round and pluck blackberries."

Elizabeth Barrett Browning

The grass in the garden behind our house in Ireland takes ten minutes to cut with a strimmer. I'm not that fast—our garden is that small. After I cut it, I put the strimmer away in a tiny shed surrounded by raised beds of roses, jasmine, blueberries, herbs, and a passionflower vine that blooms every year with an otherworldly triple-flower. I never put the strimmer away for long though. This is Ireland. The grass never dies, and it never stops growing. It just slows down a bit for Christmas holidays. In the spring, we bury tiny flower seeds in rows of pots and make sure they have a drink every day. In the summer, they bloom into glorious profusion, and everything in the garden spreads so abundantly that we have to use the pruning shears just to keep the path clear. There is work involved in tending our garden, providing what each plant needs, but it's nothing compared to the colourful sights, rich aromas and delicious flavours the garden provides us with.

In the corner, beside the bench, we have a memory tree. When I look at it, I remember the day our six-year-old son asked about the pit in his supermarket plum. When we told him that the wrinkled stone in his hand could actually become a whole new plum tree, his eyes went wide and he asked, "Can we plant it?" We hadn't thought of that, but why not? So we did. And ever since, that plum tree has been growing along with our roses and blueberries and children. It's taller than we are now, and it makes flowers that could, in the right conditions, become new plums with new wrinkled stones that could become whole new plum trees.

After God divided the land and sea on the third day of creation, he said, "'Let the land produce vegetation: seed-bearing plants and trees on the land that bear fruit with seed in it, according to their various kinds.' And it was so. The land produced vegetation: plants bearing seed according to their kinds and trees bearing fruit with seed in it according to their kinds. And God saw that it was good. And there was evening, and there was morning—the third day" (Genesis 1:11-13).

Discovering Plants

God made our world a garden. He didn't just give us rocks and soil and sand, as amazing as all those materials can be. He made the land sprout and grow with life, reaching down into the soil and up into the sky—splitting rocks, producing oxygen, and growing pineapples. So far, we've identified more than 350,000 species of plants, and that doesn't account for a further 150,000 species of fungi (which is somewhat alarming). We're still discovering more. The world God gave us is a garden world, growing wildly. Is God's favourite colour green? I don't know, but it's clear in Genesis 1 that there's one aspect of plants that he definitely wanted to draw our attention to: the word "seed" shows up four times in the space of two verses (v 11-12). That's quite a few seeds.

Have you ever thought about what's inside a seed? It's a container too small to hold much of anything—except the potential to become something. God packs life into small packages. Each seed holds the complete DNA blueprints for a whole new plant, along with all of the other microscopic machinery necessary to read those plans and carry them out. And to help the process get started, these baby plant embryos are usually accompanied by a food package from their mothers (I used to get those in university, too), and a hard shell for protection. When conditions are right, they grow. When they grow enough, they pass their life on to the next generation of seeds.

Seeds hold a power that we, with all our progress and technology, have not been able to replicate: the power of life. We can manipulate that life where we find it, promoting the traits we like and artificially modifying the DNA, but we still don't have a technique for making something come alive in the first place. We can't even do this for organic material that used to be alive, like Frankenstein's Monster or Frankenstein's Neglected Houseplant. All the structures of life might be there, but how do we make them function again? How do we make their cells divide and grow and photosynthesise energy out of sunlight and air? For all that we know about living things, the fundamental reality that anything in the universe is alive at all is still mysterious. Meanwhile, our planet grows and grows, and we don't have time to think about that mystery because we have to cut the grass.

Interpreting Plants

God didn't have to make plants grow from seeds. He chose to. He placed the most precious gift of all—life itself—in the smallest, most unimpressive of packages and scattered it everywhere. Do you find that surprising? If so, you might be surprised too that he also said his glorious eternal kingdom begins and grows like a seed (Matthew 13:31-32). All of its growth comes through a message, scattered in the world like seed sown in a field, with the power to grow in the soil of our hearts and to bear abundant fruit (v 1-23). What is this message that has such life-giving power in it? It is the gospel—the message of how Jesus himself became like a seed, and died and was buried like a seed because "unless a grain of wheat falls to the ground and dies, it remains only a single seed. But if it dies, it produces many seeds" (John 12:24). Jesus "fell to the ground and died" so that he could "produce many seeds". Now his life is spreading and growing all over the world by the power of his Spirit at work in the hearts of people from every tribe, tongue, kingdom and nation who hear and respond to the good news of his salvation. That's why the apostle Paul gave his all to preach this life-giving good news to everyone he could, and he never lost sight of where the growth really came from:

> *What, after all, is Apollos? And what is Paul? Only servants, through whom you came to believe—as the Lord has assigned to each his task. I planted the seed, Apollos watered it, but God has been making it grow. So neither the one who plants nor the one who waters is anything, but only God, who makes things grow. The one who plants and the one who waters have one purpose, and they will each be rewarded according to their own labour. For we are fellow workers in God's service; you are God's field.* (1 Corinthians 3:5-9)

Like a good farmer, Paul saw that when he shared the message of the gospel with other people, he was planting a seed. It may have looked small and insignificant to some—just words about trusting and following a man who had died and risen again—but Paul knew that this message contained the power of life. He knew how it could take root in even the hardest of human hearts (like his own) to send out shoots in their minds and to bear glorious, joyful fruit in their lives. He knew that life was something he couldn't create by himself, but he could plant the right seed, and if it had the right conditions, it would grow. And grow. And grow.

The final result of God's life growing in a human heart is more spectacular than our wildest dreams. Could you ever imagine a sunflower in all its glory just by looking at the seed? An oak tree just by looking at an acorn? Neither can you imagine what God has in store for those who love him (1 Corinthians 2:9). When Jesus died like a seed and three days later cracked the grave with his unstoppable life, he rose with the power to transform our planted graveyards into the glorious gardens of eternity (15:36-44).

Responding to Plants

If you want to live fully and abundantly, as you were made to live, you must start with the right seed—the seed that really has life in it. It's no good planting dead things, no matter how nice they are, or expensive or impressive. A clever philosophical system won't bring us real spiritual life any more than a gardening book buried in the ground will feed us. A steady diet of slick entertainment and expensive toys won't make us grow any more than a well-produced farming documentary will yield a harvest. If we're looking for real life that powers real growth, and results in real fruit that slowly but surely changes everything inside us and around us, we have to look to the right source.

There is an abundance of life in our world, but there is only one Source, and he packed the power of his life into the seed of the gospel of Jesus Christ. Now he invites you to draw life from him through it, "like a tree planted by streams of water, which yields its fruit in season and whose leaf does not wither" (Psalm 1:3). Be aware: if you accept the seed of life from the hand of God, don't be surprised if it grows in ways that you never expected. This seed will break your heart. Its roots will push down and slowly shatter the rocky places inside you—your selfishness, your pride and anger and lust and greed and vanity. And as it grows down, it will also grow up, sending shoots into the air and filling them with the aromatic flowers and delicious fruits of God's Spirit: of "love, joy, peace, forbearance, kindness, goodness, faithfulness, gentleness and self-control" (Galatians 5:22-23). These are the natural overflow of the life God pours into his own children, as a vine pours into its own branches (John 15:5). That's why Jesus doesn't tell us to simply *try harder* but to "remain in me", because "apart from me you can do nothing" (v 15). This is how we receive true spiritual life and how we grow: we come to him and remain in him. Our God is the God of all life, from the tiniest seed to the tallest sequoia. In the end, he will make his people stand strong and firm as "oaks of righteousness, a planting of the LORD for the display of his splendour" (Isaiah 61:3).

CHAPTER 10

The Rhythm
of Time

"Sunrise, sunset,
Sunrise, sunset,
Swiftly fly the years,
One season following another,
Laden with happiness and tears."

Fiddler on the Roof

O ur own garden might be small, but it's not too far away from Fota House, a stately old manor that has been restored as a tourist attraction, along with its extensive pleasure gardens. They are not small. Fota is the kind of place where it would seem perfectly natural to see Mr. Darcy strolling by with Elizabeth Bennet or awkwardly proposing to her under one of the big, spreading oak trees. Those trees are pictures of solid, sheltering stability. They started as just acorns though. Seeds. An acorn isn't nearly as good a backdrop for a proposal, but it can become one. You just have to be patient.

As the seasons change, the trees and flowers in the Fota gardens change with them. Some of the change is imperceptible, like the oak trees quietly adding one more ring of growth beneath their bark. Other changes are obvious, and we have learned to anticipate them. In the beginning of the year, the daffodils push their way out of the cold soil, and we know that spring is just around the corner. In March, we keep a close eye on the magnolias—we want to be sure to catch them while their branches are covered in flowers, before the leaves come out. After that, it's time to visit the long stone wall that's completely covered with one enormous wisteria vines, whose cascading purple flowers fill the air with fragrance. Then the roses appear and the bleeding heart flowers and the fuchsias and the wild flowers in the grass. By the autumn, most of those have begun to fade, but we come back anyway for a different kind of colour—the red, yellow, golden glory of leaves igniting and falling to the ground like slow-motion fireworks. Even in the winter there's white bark on the birch trees and orange branches on the Siberian dogwoods and evergreens that show off their bright-red berries. As the days and weeks and months pass by, the rhythm of time creates a never-ending series of glorious displays in the garden.

On the fourth day, "God said, 'Let there be lights in the vault of the sky to separate the day from the night, and let them serve as signs to mark sacred times, and days and years, and let them be lights in the vault of the sky to give light on the earth.' And it was so. God made two great lights—the greater light to govern the day and the lesser light to govern the night. He also made the stars. God set them in the vault of the sky to give light on the earth, to govern the day and the night, and to separate light from darkness. And God saw that it was good. And there was evening, and there was morning—the fourth day" (Genesis 1:14-19).

Discovering the Rhythm of Time

In the beginning, God spent a whole day of creation marking out the time he invented for us. He gave us a moon that is the perfect size and distance to cycle through clear phases of waxing and waning, becoming a giant month-clock in the sky for us. He also set the stars in order and gave us a year-long rotating view of them. He tilted our planet just enough to make the angle of the sun's light change over time, giving us summer and winter solstices and creating four distinct seasons in temperate zones, on a repeating cycle of 365 individual days.

Each year cycles through the same seasons. But in every cycle, some of the plants around us are new, some are more mature, and some are gone. Every year, some small human faces will blow dandelion seeds across the grass for the first time, while others who took in decades of cherry blossoms will miss them for the first time. The rhythm of time may look repetitive, but it never actually circles back to the same place. It only spirals forward—always forward. They tell us that history repeats itself, and in some ways that's true but never completely. The faces are always different. The trees and flowers and animals are different. Today is different from yesterday, and it will never be repeated. The sun and moon rise and fall to remind us that time is moving on—and when time moves, all of creation moves with it.

Every spring, millions of monarch butterflies leave their winter hideaway in the Sierra Madre mountains of Mexico and begin a journey north to Canada. They never make it. The journey is too long to be completed in their short lives. Their children pick up where they left off flying north, always north, but they don't make it either. The next generation also dies without a sight of their destination. Only the great-great-great-grandchildren of the original monarchs will lay their compound eyes on the glories of Canada. Humanity is on a similar journey. We are traveling through time like butterflies heading to Canada, and many generations have travelled this earth before us to bring us to where we are now. Their part in the drama of history is over, but history itself is not. It is still going, still drawing us on, leading us somewhere. The journey is longer than our lifetimes, but there is a destination.

Interpreting Times and Seasons

As we reflected in the previous chapter, every seed planted in the ground is going somewhere—and it follows the rhythm of time to get there. Jesus said that his eternal kingdom is heading in the same direction: "This is what the kingdom of God is like. A man scatters seed on the ground. Night and day, whether he sleeps or gets up, the seed sprouts and grows, though he does not know how. All by itself the soil produces corn—first the stalk, then the ear, then the full grain in the ear. As soon as the corn is ripe, he puts the sickle to it, because the harvest has come" (Mark 4:26-29). There is a harvest coming. There is a time when the work of planting and growing God's kingdom on earth will be finished: when he will separate the wheat from the weeds and gather his people to himself for eternity, like a farmer gathering his harvest (Matthew 13:36-43). Until then, there is work to be done, and there is waiting. God's life-giving seed has to be scattered, and it needs time to grow through nights and days of slow maturing— "first the stalk, then the head, then the full kernel in the head."

Even now, God is waiting, watching and tending his harvest, patiently delaying his final judgment on evil so that the seed of the gospel can grow and bear the fruit of faith in the hearts of more people (2 Peter 3:9). That's the season we're in. It is the season of salvation (2 Corinthians 6:1-2). Will we also be patient? The harvest will be worth it. James 5:7-8 tells us to "be patient, then, brothers and sisters, until the Lord's coming. See how the farmer waits for the land to yield its valuable crop, patiently waiting for the autumn and spring rains. You too, be patient and stand firm, because the Lord's coming is near." When our timeless God created a timeline for us, he gave us the context we need to experience his patience and to display it in our own lives. Time is a context that can cultivate and reveal other virtues as well. God has ordered our world so that "there is a time for everything, and a season for every activity under the heavens" (Ecclesiastes 3:1). These seasons can test and display the reality of our faith, as we trust that God's character and promises will hold before we can see how (Hebrews 11). Our faith, then, leads to courage—the virtue of looking uncertainty in the eye and taking the first step into an unknown future (Joshua 1:9). Endurance is shown in taking the second step, and the third and the 97th, with the same courage and faith and hope that led us to take the first (James 1:2-4). Then, finally, the day will come when endurance is no longer needed—when faith will become sight and promises reach fulfilment; seasons of suffering and uncertainty will turn to never-ending joy and glory as the night gives way to an everlasting day (Isaiah 60:19). Until then, we can say with David, "I trust in you, LORD; I say, 'You are my God.' My times are in your hands" (Psalm 31:14-15).

Responding to Time

There is a glory in the waiting, the striving, the growing and depending and learning and fighting our way forward that simply could not exist without a timeline. Peter wrote that trials "come so that the proven genuineness of your faith—of greater worth than gold, which perishes even though refined by fire—may result in praise, glory and honour when Jesus Christ is revealed" (1 Peter 1:7). Paul wrote that "our light and momentary troubles are achieving for us an eternal glory that far outweighs them all. So we fix our eyes not on what is seen, but on what is unseen, since what is seen is temporary, but what is unseen is eternal" (2 Corinthians 4:17-18). How do we keep a hopeful perspective in the winter cold when everything looks dead around us? We remember that spring is coming soon. How do we keep this perspective in a world that is groaning under the curse of sin? We remember that "our salvation is nearer now than when we first believed. The night is nearly over; the day is almost here. So let us put aside the deeds of darkness and put on the armour of light" (Romans 13:11-12). And with this in mind, "Let us not become weary in doing good, for at the proper time we will reap a harvest if we do not give up" (Galatians 6:9).

Today may seem like one more ordinary day, just like so many others, but it is unique. It is a day we can use to grow closer to God, as an oak tree quietly deepens its roots and expands its trunk. It is a day we can use to scatter and water gospel seed, like a farmer working towards harvest. It is a day God put us here, on Planet Earth, "for such a time as this" (Esther 4:14). Today we have the privilege of being alive, being part of the story of history. As we look up and see the sun and moon rising and setting and waxing and waning above us, we can let them remind us that time is moving on, and that when time moves, we must move with it: forward, always forward, in faith, in hope, in courage and endurance. We are not marching in circles. We're going somewhere.

Those who sow with tears
*   will reap with songs of joy.*
Those who go out weeping,
*   carrying seed to sow,*
will return with songs of joy,
*   carrying sheaves with them.*   *(Psalm 126:5-6)*

CHAPTER 11

Naming
the Stars

*"If people sat outside and looked at the stars each
night, I'll bet they'd live a lot differently."*

Bill Watterson

As I step outside into the night, the moon catches
my eye first. Its rocky surface is bright with the
reflected light of the sun, but it is not alone. The
blanket of darkness around it is broken with countless
pinhole points of light—countless burning balls of fire,
each one powerful enough to destroy everything I know
and love, but all of them so far away that they only burn
like distant candles in the windows of heaven.

Heaven has a lot of candles. I start counting them, but
I lose track before I even have to shift my eyes. I shake
my head and decide that Genesis 1:16 is one of the most
extreme understatements in the history of language:
"God made two great lights—the greater light to govern
the day and the lesser light to govern the night. He

also made the stars." That's it. In the same chapter where tiny seeds are highlighted four times, the entire universe of stars is thrown in as an aside. Stars! Literally the biggest part of creation, barely mentioned. Then again, did he need to elaborate? The stars are already pouring forth speech.

Discovering Stars

Our local star, the sun, is so big that it could fit more than a million earths inside it. That's impressive, but there's another star in our galaxy that we call UY Scuti (who names these things?) that could fit five billion suns inside it. That's just one of somewhere around 100 billion stars in the Milky Way. Or maybe 400 billion. We're not sure. It's a lot though, and that's just one galaxy. In 1995, NASA aimed the Hubble Space Telescope at what looked like a gap of empty space between visible stars. The images that came back were bursting with light—not from individual stars but from scores of distant galaxies. After that, our estimates about the number of galaxies had to be multiplied by ten. We're into the trillions now, and every one of those galaxies could contain 100 billion stars, or maybe 400 billion stars, and if you put all of that together, it adds up to this: you can't imagine how many stars there are. All we've really proved so far is that every time we invent a better telescope, we find more of them. Only God knows how many there really are. Psalm 147:4 tells us that "he determines the number of the stars and calls them each by name". Can you imagine? I'll bet his names sound better than UY Scuti.

He must still be naming them because new stars are born every day. This universe we're in is not only mind-bogglingly massive—it's growing. So even as we work to design better telescopes to see galaxies further away from us, the galaxies we'd like to see are moving further away. Fast. We have no idea how far the universe goes beyond the light we see. All we really know is that the universe we live in is enormous beyond comprehension and beyond observation, and we, by comparison, are very, very small.

Interpreting Stars

A being who can create stars and galaxies beyond counting must be incredibly powerful and bigger than our minds can conceive. He must be wise, as well, to invent the laws that govern these galaxies so well. It seems excessive, though—wouldn't one galaxy be more than enough to overwhelm us with his power and wisdom? Of course it would, but the scale of the universe is not calibrated to humanity. God is infinite. If he wanted to paint a picture of what infinity actually means, that picture would look like our universe. If there's an edge, we'll never see it. The whole expanse is expanding constantly. And our view of the greatness of our Creator should do the exact same thing: expand constantly.

While the existence of the universe settles the question of God's majesty conclusively, it raises another question: isn't a God like this far too big and distant and powerful to notice the inhabitants of one tiny planet? If you tried to interpret the stars without the Rosetta Stone of God's word, this would be a logical conclusion.

In fact, this very question is raised in Scripture by King David, who said:

When I consider your heavens,
the work of your fingers,
the moon and the stars,
which you have set in place,
what is mankind that you are mindful of them,
human beings that you care for them?

(Psalm 8:3-4)

The magnitude of God's creative power in the stars is supposed to overwhelm us, but that's not where the Bible stops in interpreting their meaning. It goes further—overwhelming us once again with the thought that a God this big would take an interest in people like us. When David asks, *What are human beings that you care for them?* he is asking *why* a God like this would care, not whether he does; he already knows from history, God's word and his personal experience that God does, in fact, care about us. A lot. The Bible gives us a surprising interpretation of the stars because they are not only made to remind us of God's power. They are made to remind us of how God uses his power on behalf of the tiny inhabitants of Planet Earth. In the same psalm that says God "determines the number of the stars and calls them each by name", the verse immediately before has just said that "he heals the broken-hearted and binds up their wounds" (Psalm 147:3-4). Would a God who can fling out galaxies by the trillions actually stoop to bind up the broken heart of one teensy little person on one tiny little planet? Yes. Remember, he doesn't just fling out stars—he knows their names. He doesn't just populate a planet with humans—he carefully and individually crafts each one of us (139:13-18). He knows the condition of your heart right now. And he cares. When we look at the vast expanse of the heavens above us, this is the message we're meant to hear:

Lift up your eyes and look to the heavens:
who created all these?
He who brings out the starry host one by one
and calls forth each of them by name.
Because of his great power and mighty strength,
not one of them is missing.

Why do you complain, Jacob?
Why do you say, Israel,
"My way is hidden from the LORD;
my cause is disregarded by my God"?

Do you not know?
Have you not heard?
The LORD is the everlasting God,
the Creator of the ends of the earth.
He will not grow tired or weary,
and his understanding no one can fathom.
He gives strength to the weary
and increases the power of the weak.
Even youths grow tired and weary,
and young men stumble and fall;
but those who hope in the LORD
will renew their strength.
They will soar on wings like eagles;

> *they will run and not grow weary,*
> *they will walk and not be faint.* (Isaiah 40:26-31)

If God can account for each and every star by name, then he can also account for the details of your life. If he is strong enough to uphold each and every star by his power, then he is strong enough to uphold his children. Will we really look up into the eyes of the Maker of the stars and say, "I don't think you can handle my problems"? Will we really imagine that the Creator of galaxies cannot keep his promises?

Responding to Stars

The God of the numberless stars is bigger than we can imagine, but he is not distant. He is here, right now, right where you are. King David—the same king who asked the question of Psalm 8—also wrote a celebration of God's presence in Psalm 139:7-10:

> *Where can I go from your Spirit?*
> *Where can I flee from your presence?*
> *If I go up to the heavens, you are there;*
> *if I make my bed in the depths, you are there.*
> *If I rise on the wings of the dawn,*
> *if I settle on the far side of the sea,*
> *even there your hand will guide me,*
> *your right hand will hold me fast.*

Whether you recognise his presence or not, he is near. And he acts through his creation and the story of history so that people will "seek him and perhaps reach out for him and find him, though he is not far from any one of us" (Acts 17:27). He is the God of the galaxies, and he is the God of kitchens, creeks, cubicles and caves. He is ready to be found by anyone who will simply turn and seek him, as he promises in Jeremiah 29:13: "You will seek me and find me when you seek me with all your heart". In finding him, we find everything. The God of the boundless universe promises to bless his children with boundless blessings—not just the #blessed blessings that most people think of; those blessings are nice, but they are countable, like the stars in our neighbourhood at the edge of one of the spiral arms of the Milky Way. When God talks about blessing his people, he has more in mind—much more. He doesn't just give his children a few good presents; he gives them himself (Luke 11:13). No other blessing can compare. They are just drops. He is the fountain (John 4:13-14).

The God of the universe promises to be with his children who trust in him. The God who made the stars—with us! And he said that nothing in the universe—not even death itself—would be able to separate us from his love (Romans 8:31-39). He has assured us that he is preparing a place for us in heaven (John 14:1-3), and that we will live there with him for ever. It's hard to imagine what for ever is like, but if the universe teaches us anything, it teaches us that eternity can never be boring if it's spent with the infinite God. We could never finish exploring our ever-expanding universe. And how much more is there to discover in the God who made it? For ever is not long enough, but we can—and should—start now. The God of the heavens has stooped to open his arms and welcome us close to himself. Our response should always be to run into them as quickly as possible, trusting ourselves and our lives and our everything to the God who numbers, names and upholds the stars.

CHAPTER 12

The Mysteries
of the Deep

*"The sea is an underwater museum still
awaiting its visitors."*

Philippe Diolé

A small fishing boat was bobbing on the gentle waves
of Cork harbour, and our family was bobbing with
it. It was a good day to be out on the water with a
friend—not a good day for catching fish. But we were
enjoying the company, the open sky and the water
around us. After leaving our hooks in one spot for a
while, we'd motor on to another and put them down
again, fruitlessly. By late afternoon, it was time to go
home. As we crossed the mouth of the harbour once
more, the water was broken from beneath and a fin
emerged—a dolphin, breaching right beside us. Before
we could finish saying, "Did you see that?" and "Wasn't
that amazing?" it happened again. And again. All of
a sudden, we were surrounded by a pod of dolphins

breaking the waves and—some of them—leaping into the air. We turned off the engine and floated in awed silence, watching the dance unfold around us. Finally, our visitors returned to the depths, working together to catch the fish that we hadn't. We'd caught something else that day—a glimpse of the living world beneath the waves.

On the fifth day of creation, "God said, 'Let the water teem with living creatures, and let birds fly above the earth across the vault of the sky.' So God created the great creatures of the sea and every living thing with which the water teems and that moves about in it, according to their kinds, and every winged bird according to its kind. And God saw that it was good. God blessed them and said, 'Be fruitful and increase in number and fill the water in the seas, and let the birds increase on the earth.' And there was evening, and there was morning—the fifth day" (Genesis 1:20-23).

Discovering Sea Creatures

Star Trek may call space the "final frontier", but that fictional future isn't our current reality. Even as we send more and more telescopes and probes into outer space, we still have another frontier to discover much closer to home. Beneath the chaotic surface of Earth's oceans, there is a world of mysteries we have only begun to unravel. While our satellites and probes and rovers have been able to map the surface of Mars almost entirely, most of our own ocean floor remains unknown and uncharted. Oceans cover most of our own planet, but we've only managed to physically explore about 5% of their depths.

As little as we've seen of it, we already know quite well that when God said, "Let the water teem with living creatures", he meant it. The ocean depths are filled with life—not only in astonishing numbers but also in variety so great that we are constantly finding new forms of it. We've already categorised more species of fish with backbones than all other vertebrate species combined—including all mammals, birds, reptiles and amphibians. And fish only make up about an eighth of all the living species of creatures we've discovered teeming in the ocean. Every year, we discover thousands more, like the fluffy sponge crab, which we never noticed before because it uses a bit of sponge for a hat; or the golden cloak anemone, which gets along so well with its hermit-crab host that when the crab moves to a bigger shell, it makes sure to move the anemone with it. How many more species like these are there? There could be millions. We simply don't know.

What we do know is that God made shining scales in every conceivable size, pattern and colour. He made octopuses that can change colour and move with jet propulsion. He made sharks that never stop swimming and floating blobs of jelly with their portable party-streamer tentacles. Or that's what they look like—smaller fish who try to join that party might find themselves on the hors d'oeuvres list. In the dark depths of trenches, where rigid bodies like ours would be crushed instantly under incredible pressure, God made anglerfish, which swim freely with bioluminescent lures and mouths and bodies so pliable that they can swallow prey twice as big as themselves. And while on land unicorns may only exist in storybooks, in the water there are narwhals wearing their horns. There are eels that can generate electricity. There are blue whales that survive on a diet of tiny krill and yet grow bigger than any dinosaur. There are immortal jellyfish that don't die of old age because they can choose to revert to their juvenile form as many times as they like. There are mantis shrimp that can see ultraviolet and polarised light that is invisible to our eyes. There are nautili and nudibranchs and sea dragons that make the imaginations of sci-fi and fantasy writers seem provincial and quaint. And that's just the creatures we know about.

Interpreting Sea Creatures

Creation may be pouring forth speech, as Psalm 19 says, but our ears have a harder time hearing clearly underwater. We're not used to the thickness of it, or the weightlessness it creates. Understanding and interpreting what God is saying to us through a world of creatures who are living in an environment so foreign to our own takes more effort. If God is speaking to us through creation, why did he make some of his language so hard to hear? Why did he hide so many of his creative wonders in such inaccessible places that we may never even see them? In our age of self-expression and viral videos and influencers, this seems counterproductive. Isn't the whole point of putting effort and skill into something to get credit for it? And to get credit, your work has to be noticed. In our human systems of measuring work, the people who are noticed most are the people whose work is considered most valuable. It doesn't even have to be the best work—if it's the most widely known, it gains more value simply for being more known. In our system, hidden work—however skilful it is—is hardly valued at all.

God doesn't use our system. He does his work in ways that are different from what we are used to, and he does it with different priorities (Isaiah 55:8-9). As Proverbs 25:2 says, "It is the glory of God to conceal a matter; to search out a matter is the glory of kings". Our God is a God who purposefully hides some of his creative work. We're not used to this kind of behaviour—which means we need to pay attention to it even more.

> *How many are your works, LORD!*
>   *In wisdom you made them all;*
>   *the earth is full of your creatures.*
> *There is the sea, vast and spacious,*
>   *teeming with creatures beyond number—*
>   *living things both large and small.*
> (Psalm 104:24-25)

The psalmist didn't feel the need to categorise each of the Lord's works individually before he appreciated the wisdom and abundance of God's creativity. In fact, the knowledge that there are "creatures beyond number"—beyond our counting and classifying—only amplifies his praise. God has the power to work wonders far beyond the borders of our human abilities or understanding. Knowing that there is more that moves in the sea than we understand, more than we can categorise or control, should help us remember that the God who created these marvels is himself more than we can know, understand, categorise or control. That was God's point to Job when he asked if Job could tame the giant monsters of the ocean, or if he had "journeyed to the springs of the sea or walked in the recesses of the deep?" (Job 38:16). One of the reasons why it is "the glory of God to conceal a matter" is because we need to remember that we have yet to come to the end of discovering who he is. This calls for humility. There are always more mysteries for us to uncover, but God sees through every one of them and acts with perfect knowledge in every corner of creation.

> The LORD does whatever pleases him,
>   in the heavens and on the earth,
>   in the seas and all their depths.   *(Psalm 135:6)*

On the fifth day of creation, it pleased God to fill the ocean with "creatures beyond number". And now, it pleases him to "give them their food at the proper time" (104:27) and continually renew their numbers (v 30). Our God not only creates the hidden creatures of the deep; he also sustains them—just as he upholds the numberless stars. He is a God of power and creativity beyond the edges of what we see, and a God of detailed provision beyond the borders of our notice. "It is the glory of God to conceal a matter." The teeming life of the sea is glorious—even the life that is unknown to anyone but God alone.

Responding to Sea Creatures

"To search out a matter is the glory of kings" (Proverbs 25:2)—what God has hidden, it is our privilege to discover. It is a joy to search out the mysteries of God's creation and to let them unfold a greater understanding of the God behind them all—the God who can imagine giant squids, playful dolphins and colourful coral. And as we discover his works, we should be encouraged that the God who sees every lanternfish in the deep darkness and cares for every faceless fish in the Mariana Trench also sees us and our work.

Are there times when you feel that your life is too hidden to matter? Too unnoticed to mean anything? Let the ocean full of hidden creatures remind you that God sees what others miss and that our hidden obedience and faith also bring glory to God. Jesus himself told us to imitate our Father, who purposefully hides so much of his work. He said that our giving to others should be done in secret—not to be rewarded by people but to be seen and rewarded by God (Matthew 6:4). He said the same thing about our prayers (v 6) and fasting (v 18). If we live our lives and do our work primarily to be seen by others, he said that the glory we receive from them will be our only reward. This is, of course, exactly the reward that the world around us seeks constantly: the glory of others, the power of influence, the satisfaction of a large, devoted following. All of these things do have a kind of glory, but it is only the glory of the shallows—the turbulent, changeable and temporary glory that is given (and taken) by temporary creatures. Meanwhile, God is calling us into the deep water of knowing him. He is calling us to live our lives and do our work in his sight, whether anyone else notices or not. Like God's creation, our lives should also have depths that are not immediately seen by everyone around us. There ought to be more to us than meets the eye: a deeper relationship with God, a quiet depth of character, a joy in hidden obedience that is offered freely to the God who sees to the bottom of every ocean and every heart. Don't worry if others fail to notice your work. God sees what they don't. He rewards in ways that they can't. A hidden life that is devoted to the Lord can be as deep and glorious as the sea.

CHAPTER 13

The Freedom of the Skies

"A new day was starting, the things of the garden were not concerned with our troubles. A blackbird ran across the rose-garden to the lawns in swift, short rushes, stopping now and again to stab at the earth with his yellow beak. A thrush, too, went about his business, and two stout, little wagtails, following one another, and a little cluster of twittering sparrows. A gull poised himself high in the air, silent and alone, and then spread his wings wide and swooped beyond the lawns to the woods and the Happy Valley. These things continued, our worries and anxieties had no power to alter them."

Daphne du Maurier, in *Rebecca*

From the flat summit of the highest mound, I could see the layout of the lost city below me. The hot Georgia sun made the sweat drip into my eyes, but I brushed it aside and tried to imagine the buildings and streets and people and lives that this land once held. Situated on the banks of the Ocmulgee River, this area had been a thriving centre of Native American civilisation for thousands of years. Even today, you can see how the inhabitants shaped the earth—an enormous temple mound still rises at one end of the site, with several smaller mounds below it. One of these man-made hills even has a doorway in it, leading into a large, round underground room. When I went inside, I saw millennium-old seats carved around the perimeter of the hardened clay floor. At the furthest end, one seat rose slightly above the rest, within the outline of an enormous bird that was shaped into the ground. In the council room under the hill, an ancient chief had intentionally identified his position with birds.

Things have changed—but not so much. The current chief of North America sits in an office on top of a hill, but the floor in front of him is similarly decorated with a large picture of a bird. A bald eagle, specifically—a symbol of freedom and strength. And why not? Why wouldn't you want to identify yourself and your nation with a creature that rises above everything and soars in the air with complete freedom?

On the day God filled the sea with life, he also filled the sky:

God said, "Let the water teem with living creatures, and let birds fly above the earth across the vault of the sky." So God created the great creatures of the sea and every living thing with which the water teems and that moves about in it, according to their kinds, and every winged bird according to its kind. And God saw that

*it was good. God blessed them and said, 'Be fruitful
and increase in number and fill the water in the seas,
and let the birds increase on the earth.' And there was
evening, and there was morning—the fifth day.*

(Genesis 1:20-23)

Discovering Birds

Wilbur and Orville Wright are widely believed to have
become the first humans to invade the domain of
birds on 17th December, 1903. Since then, air travel
has become commonplace for humans, drastically
reducing travel times around the world and granting us
a far greater freedom of movement. And yet, for all the
advances we've made in roaming the sky, we're still a
long way from the freedom of birds.

Watch a songbird approach a tree—it doesn't need
a long runway to land on. It doesn't need permission
from air-traffic control. A tiny twig will do the job,
for as long as it likes to linger. It might stay to sing a
song, and then it's off again, in whatever direction it
chooses. Eagles make their homes in the high cliffs of
mountains, virtually unapproachable by land, and did
any fortified castle ever boast a more formidable wall?
Bar-tailed godwits can migrate all the way from Alaska
to New Zealand in a single non-stop, eight-day flight.
Yes, that's longer than it would take in a plane, but they
don't need a ticket, a pilot, or a flying machine—they
are a flying machine.

Unlike our aircraft, birds fly without the help of
engines. Their wings are agile, able to move and push
against the air to provide the upward thrust that we

refine jet fuel for. During flight, birds can adjust the shape of their wings to reduce drag and maximise lift, glide effortlessly in air currents, respond to turbulence, suddenly change direction, or dive for prey. I once saw a mother swallow flying at full speed straight through a crack that was hardly bigger than herself above the door of a shed. There's not a stunt pilot or plane on earth that could manage that trick and land as she did on the other side. But the swallow wasn't trying to impress me—she was just bringing food to her hungry children.

If you had the swallow's wings in your own size, you still wouldn't be able to fly. Your muscles aren't designed to use wings, and your bones are too heavy. The bones of birds are hollow, as are their feathers, to achieve maximum strength at minimum weight. Their various kinds of feathers work together to create perfectly shaped wings, able to harness the power of the wind and provide warmth and protection from the elements. And as they soar and sing, many birds also fill the air with glorious colours. God was not content to leave the sky empty. He filled it with living creatures of astonishing beauty, incredible design, and—what makes us most envious—boundless freedom.

Interpreting Birds

One of the greatest symbols of freedom in the world is a bird on the wing. It has no restraints; it owns the sky—not even gravity can keep it down. The bird can go where it wishes, when it wishes, and no one can stop it. It's little wonder that its wings have become a symbol of unrestricted liberty. Did God create birds simply to taunt us with a level of freedom we can never attain? No. I think one of the reasons he made them was to teach us what real freedom looks like.

While we may see birds as a symbol of complete independence, God's word tells us to look more closely and see that birds actually live in complete dependence on the provision of their Maker. Jesus encouraged us to trust in his provision like the birds do, in Matthew 6:25-27:

> *Therefore I tell you, do not worry about your life,*
> *what you will eat or drink; or about your body, what*
> *you will wear. Is not life more than food, and the body*
> *more than clothes? Look at the birds of the air; they do*
> *not sow or reap or store away in barns, and yet your*
> *heavenly Father feeds them. Are you not much more*
> *valuable than they? Can any one of you by worrying*
> *add a single hour to your life?*

So nature's greatest picture of freedom does not live in independence but in the greater freedom of worry-free dependence on God. This dependence is not merely for food—think of how birds fly, of where they go, and why. Even their longest flights are not aimless or chosen independently. Birds migrate according to the seasons and the needs of their species, following the order God made for them, which is something the Bible tells us we should learn from:

> *Even the stork in the sky*
> *knows her appointed seasons,*
> *and the dove, the swift and the thrush*

> *observe the time of their migration.*
> *But my people do not know*
> *the requirements of the* LORD.   *(Jeremiah 8:7)*

The birds in the heavens are free like no other creature, but they don't decide individually which way they would like to go for the winter. They know instinctively that God's order is right for them, and they freely follow it. We humans are the ones who get confused on that point. Nature's embodiment of freedom not only lives in dependence on God but also in obedience to him.

A few years ago, we had the opportunity to watch two blue tits take up residence in a birdhouse outside our kitchen window. Every day we saw them coming and going, going and coming, coming and constantly going. They certainly made good use of their wings! And every time they came back, they had more bits of straw and grass and twigs for their nest. Then, after the nest was finished, one of the birds stopped coming out. Instead, she sat for weeks inside the birdhouse on her eggs. Meanwhile, Dad was doing double-time; he was running for food constantly, in and out, out and in, feeding both himself and Mum, bringing a steady stream of worms and grubs and such. When the babies hatched, it was an even more hectic schedule, with Mum and Dad both searching for food for their little family. Finally (and we had the delight of seeing it happen), the little ones took to their own wings and flew away. Yes, it was a wonder to see them soaring through the sky—to imagine what that must feel like. The bird is free. And where does he or she go with all that freedom? They go to get food for their family.

Even the sparrow has found a home,
  and the swallow a nest for herself,
where she may have her young.   *(Psalm 84:3)*

Responding to Birds

Somehow, we've picked up the idea that real freedom means absolute self-determination and complete independence from needing or being guided by anyone else—including God himself. This lie is as old as the snake in the Garden of Eden. In freeing ourselves from dependence on God, we only free ourselves from the one who provides "every good and perfect gift" (James 1:17). In diverting from his course, we only gain the self-made burden of trying to re-create our own direction from scratch—like a wandering bird in winter that stubbornly refuses to follow the flock to God's provided haven, or a straggler hunting for food where there is none, alone and unprotected from the predators that lurk around them.

Birds declare to us every day that there is a better kind of freedom—a freedom found in dependence on the provision and wisdom of our Creator. This is the path of true freedom. Freedom from worry, from self-obsession and from the aimless, lonely search for direction. Freedom to trust, follow, share and enjoy the provision of God. And I really do mean enjoy—don't the birds sing every day?

This joy and security is not only for us. As we enjoy the freedom of depending on our dependable God, we can safely turn our attention from our own needs to the needs of others. Just as the birds outside of our kitchen window leveraged their wings to bring food to their offspring, we can leverage our own strength and freedom to provide for others out of all that God has provided for us. I can't be quite sure, but I think the birds in our garden may have been singing the words of Paul in Galatians:

You, my brothers and sisters, were called to be free. But do not use your freedom to indulge the flesh; rather, serve one another humbly in love.

(Galatians 5:13)

CHAPTER 14

More Than Meets the Eye

*"There are more things in Heaven and Earth,
Horatio, than are dreamt of in your philosophy."*

William Shakespeare, in *Hamlet*

Growing up with a dog in Possum Holler was a good recipe for a happy childhood. Cinnamon made an excellent companion when I wandered the forest on the mountain behind our house. We didn't need a destination. There was always something interesting up there—little run-off streams and rock outcroppings, sunlight through leaves, squirrels hurrying from tree to tree, and the awareness of being among innumerable living things in the presence of God. Or at least, those were the kinds of things that interested me. Cinnamon's attention was directed differently. While I explored the forest with my eyes, she explored it with her nose. The path she followed was winding and mysterious to me, because she was guided by scent trails that I could not detect. With her large, sensitive nose, she could read the world backwards, beyond the present reality that I could see and into the histories of which animals had visited those places before us and what they had done. While it seemed strange to me that she would keep her head down as we walked among so many beautiful sights, it probably seemed strange to her (if she thought about it) that her boy would ignore all the interesting stories that she was constantly uncovering. I didn't mean to ignore them. I just couldn't smell as well as she could. God equipped Cinnamon with a sense so far beyond my own that it enabled her to detect things I could only imagine. And it's not just dogs—God filled the land we inhabit with a wide variety of creatures that live and move and sense the world in ways that are very different from us.

On the sixth day, "God said, 'Let the land produce living creatures according to their kinds: the livestock, the creatures that move along the ground, and the wild animals, each according to its kind.' And it was so. God made the wild animals according to their kinds, the livestock according to their kinds, and all the creatures that move along the ground according to their kinds. And God saw that it was good" (Genesis 1:24-25).

Discovering Animals

After God filled the sea and sky with teeming life, he filled the land as well. As we look across the ground God has put us on, there are creatures of every size and description living and looking back at us. Using the categories of Genesis, some of them are "wild animals" and some are domesticated "livestock", but the biggest category of them all is the "creatures that move along the ground", because that category includes insects, and there are approximately ten quintillion of those alive on Earth at any given time. That's a lot of bugs. The range of diversity in the animal kingdom, from elephants to earwigs, really is mind-boggling—in size, structure, modes of movement, sounds, coverings and almost everything else, including the ways that they perceive the world around them. Like Cinnamon, many animals have senses that are honed to detect aspects of reality that are beyond the reach of our perception.

For the majority of humans, sight is the primary sense we use to understand and navigate the world around us. We tend to have good eyes (or in my case, good glasses), so we see the world sharply and in gorgeous colour. While most mammals have two kinds of colour-sensing cone cells collecting light in their eyes, we have three— one for detecting the spectrum of blue light, one for green light and one for red. Mammals with two kinds of colour cones (like Cinnamon) can see around 10,000 different combinations of those colours. Our ability to see a third kind of colour does not just add another few thousand to the mix—as the three spectrums of colour combine with each other, the possibilities are compounded exponentially, so that we see up to a million different shades. As beautiful and impressive as that is, it's still only a fraction of the colours that truly exist in the world. The full spectrum of colours that light creates goes beyond what human eyes can detect, into a range we call "ultraviolet" (because it's beyond the violet of the rainbow we see). What would it be like to have a fourth kind of cone in our eyes—a cone equipped to detect the colours in the ultraviolet spectrum? This is exactly the equipment that most reptiles (and many fish and birds) have in their eyes. As the ultraviolet light combines with other colours, the possibilities compound exponentially—allowing them to see 100 times more colour combinations. Can you imagine seeing 100 million shades of colour? I can't. How could we possibly know what the world looks like with a fourth spectrum of colour? Yet the colours are real. They are all around us, all the time, and many animals see them.

Colours are only the beginning. Some snakes have a special pit organ that functions like a second eye, except, instead of seeing light, it sees heat. This sense enables them to hunt with precision in complete darkness, following the warmth generated by the living creatures around them. Some of their prey have surprising defences though. Frog eggs might seem like an easy snack, but unhatched tadpoles are able to sense and recognise the specific vibrations of an attacking snake— when they feel them, they hatch immediately and slip away. Like tadpoles, elephants are also able to feel and respond to subtle vibrations in the ground that identify specific threats and relay information from nearby friends and family. It is a form of communication that is silent to us, but I won't say it's "as quiet as a mouse" because actual mice make plenty of noise. They even sing complex songs, like birds. Yes, really. The difference is that they sing in such a high ultra-sonic range that our ears are unable to discern their melodies.

All around us, the world is filled with colours, heat maps, vibrations, sounds and other sensations that animals respond to but we cannot perceive. In Africa, there are mole rats that can sense the earth's magnetic field and use it to orient their nests and find their way through the underground darkness. In Australia, duck-billed platypuses use their bills to read the electrical currents around them, and they read them so well that they can hunt with their eyes closed. Similarly, the hairs that make bees look cute and fuzzy also enable them to sense the electrical fields created by blooming flowers. Do some flowers have prettier, more appealing electrical fields? It's impossible for us to know. One thing we do know is that bees, along with most other insects and larger animals as well, communicate volumes of information to each other silently through chemical compounds known as pheromones. These chemical signposts are the reason why ants can follow a trail to food, dogs can learn everything they need to know about each other from a few sniffs, and moths can find a mate from several kilometres away. All around us, the world is bursting with messages and meanings that we are simply not equipped to detect.

Interpreting Animals

Along with the rest of creation, the animals "pour forth speech" and "declare the glory of God" (Psalm 19:1-2). Their lives are an expression of him—their diversity an outpouring of his creativity, their design a display of his wisdom (104:24). God rules the animals with perfect knowledge:

For every animal of the forest is mine,
  and the cattle on a thousand hills.
I know every bird in the mountains,
  and the insects in the fields are mine.   *(50:10-11)*

Yes, even the insects—every one of the 10 quintillion. The wide diversity of animals speaks a wide variety of messages to us about the God who made them. Many vital truths of Scripture are taught to us through references to animals—lions and lambs, sheep and goats, deer and donkeys and grasshoppers and pigs. The animal kingdom is rich with meaning—full of significant details that God meant for us to discover and respond to.

How then should we interpret the many animals that possess senses so far beyond our own that they can detect entire realms of creation that are invisible to us? The singing mice we can't hear, the magnetic mole rats, or the electric-sensitive platypuses—they all remind us powerfully that there is far more to God's creation than meets the eye (or meets our eye, anyway). It is always tempting for us to live our lives based only on the data that presents itself to our senses—pursuing pleasurable sensations, avoiding painful ones, and ignoring anything else. But the Bible joins with the mice and mole rats to remind us that there are vitally important realities beyond the borders of our senses. For example, 2 Kings chapter 6 records a time when the prophet Elisha was surrounded by an enemy army. His servant began to despair, but look at Elisha's response:

"Don't be afraid," the prophet answered. "Those who are with us are more than those who are with them." And Elisha prayed, "Open his eyes, LORD, so that he may see." Then the LORD opened the servant's eyes, and he looked and saw the hills full of horses and chariots of fire all around Elisha. (v 16-17)

The army of angels that the servant couldn't see was greater than the army of humans that were visible to him. The greatest reality of all, God himself, is invisible to our eyes (1 Timothy 1:17), yet he promises to be present with his people (Hebrews 13:5) and sends his angels "to serve those who will inherit salvation" (Hebrews 1:14). Many modern people view such claims as fantastical, akin to fairytales and make-believe, but why should they be? Why should we assume that the full scope of reality can only include things that our own senses can detect? Even the animals teach us that such assumptions are foolish.

Responding to Animals

When you step into the grass and breathe the air, you are surrounded by invisible messages written in chemicals, vibrations, and sounds too high for you to hear. You are surrounded by a host of invisible colours and acted on by powerful, invisible forces like magnetism and electricity. The next time you go outside, don't forget to consider the many realities that lie beyond your perception. Don't forget to feel the significance of the many things you can't feel, smell or touch. Don't forget to account for the importance of what is not visible.

There is more to reality than meets the eye. The animals themselves teach us this and call us to respond to their Creator and ours. Like Moses, who "persevered because he saw him who is invisible" (Hebrews 11:27), we can look beyond the hieroglyphics of creation to the Author himself. He is more real than any created reality, more glorious than any created glory and more wonderful than any created wonder. "For we live by faith, not by sight" (2 Corinthians 5:7).

CHAPTER 15

The Image of God

"The material world has latent music in it, and a renewed heart knows how to bring it out and make it vocal. Creation is the organ, and a gracious man finds out its keys, lays his hand on them, and wakes the whole system of the universe to the harmony of praise."

Charles Spurgeon

A cliff rises above the sea, jagged, wild, immovable. The waves, far below, break against it with rhythmic violence. This is where the ocean ends and the patchwork fields suddenly begin. In the fields, there are sheep. As I walk past, one of them looks up at me as it chews a disinterested mouthful of grass. It has eyes, so it can see the same view I see. It has ears, so it can hear the waves and the gulls crying out above it.

I am only visiting, and part of me envies this sheep its home and its everyday sights and sounds. I look up and wonder what the gull's eyes are seeing as it soars over all of this on the power of the wind. I wonder, if I were a gull, could I ever get used to that feeling enough to focus on feeding myself? I think I might be a skinny gull. But I think I would be filled with the thrill of wonder.

The gull I see is fat, and the sheep is too. Both are good at surviving. Both have eyes and see food clearly. They have ears and hear danger coming. But neither of them sees the beauty of their surroundings or understands how their own presence adds to it. Neither of them is comforted by the rhythmic sound of the waves like I am, or astonished by the power of the wind—not even the gull, who has wings to harness it. They live, they survive, and I do think they genuinely enjoy the comforts of soft grass and warm sunshine. But when the sun sets, they do not see the artistry in the sky—even when they look at it. They are not curious about the science of how grass seeds grow into living plants and provide food for living animals. They are not so moved by the sight of the sea as to contemplate the mysteries of existence or write poetic verses.

I've heard people say that humans are simply animals, surviving. If that were true, we would survive, but we would never travel long distances to see where the ocean ends, to hear its waves and soak in its majestic immensity. We do these things because we know that there is more to living than mere survival. There is art and beauty and meaning, mystery and discovery and wonder. The sheep don't see it. The gull doesn't see it, even with a bird's-eye view. God gave them eyes like the ones he gave you and me, but behind our eyes he gave us something more: a soul, created in his own image. The animals see and eat and live as we do, but they are not consciously aware of and able to respond and relate to the one who made these scenes and gave this life. We are.

After God created the animals on the sixth day, he finished his work with one final creation: us.

Then God said, "Let us make mankind in our image, in our likeness, so that they may rule over the fish in the sea and the birds in the sky, over the livestock and all the wild animals, and over all the creatures that move along the ground."

So God created mankind in his own image,
in the image of God he created them;
male and female he created them.

God blessed them and said to them, "Be fruitful and increase in number; fill the earth and subdue it. Rule over the fish in the sea and the birds in the sky and over every living creature that moves on the ground." Then God said, "I give you every seed-bearing plant on the face of the whole earth and every tree that has fruit with seed in it. They will be yours for food. And to all the beasts of the earth and all the birds in the sky and all the creatures that move along the ground— everything that has the breath of life in it—I give every green plant for food." And it was so. God saw all that he had made, and it was very good. And there was evening, and there was morning—the sixth day.
(Genesis 1:26-31)

Discovering Ourselves

Once upon a time, you were born into a world of wonders. After that, everything was a discovery. You discovered your hands and learned how to use them. You discovered your legs and learned how to walk. You discovered your tongue and learned how to move it in the right ways to imitate the sounds you heard from the people around you so that you could express meaning in ways that they would understand. And by using your hands and your feet and your eyes and ears and mouth and nose—whatever senses and abilities you've been given, however sharp, however limited— you also began to discover the world that God put you in. You are a human.

Out of all the incredible works that God made in the universe, and out of all the billions of living beings he filled the earth with, humanity is in the unique position of being able to hear, understand, and respond to the voice of God in the two languages he has spoken through. We see his world, and in our hearts and minds we are moved like no other creature on Earth—we are moved by the voice of God. We read his word, and the small squiggles of ink on its pages communicate truth and beauty and love and justice and salvation to our souls. Even if you only know one human language, you are still, in this sense, bilingual. You are equipped to hear and respond to God's voice in both his word and his world.

It doesn't matter that you might be the most unknown, unnoticed person on Earth; the fact that God specifically designed you to hear and understand him and equipped you to respond to him—and the further fact that he went to such great pains to communicate with you through two different languages—means that, at the very least, you must be incredibly significant. There's no other possible conclusion. The Creator of everything designed you uniquely to know him and to be known by him.

Interpreting Ourselves

Humans are the strangest hybrid to ever exist, in myth or reality. We are part spirit and part creature. A griffin makes more sense—part eagle and part lion. At least those are both animals. What are we? There's no denying that we are like the animals, with animal-like weaknesses and animal-like urges and animal-like functions. As Solomon put it, "As for humans, God tests them so that they may see that they are like the animals. Surely the fate of human beings is like that of the animals; the same fate awaits them both: as one dies, so dies the other" (Ecclesiastes 3:18-19). We are born like animals, we eat and drink and sleep like animals, and we live and die like animals. Except not quite. For if we are only animals, then we're the oddest animals that ever lived.

Animals follow instinct. A cheetah lives and survives quite well, but it never pauses to feel remorse for killing another animal's child. A female praying mantis never takes time to think through the moral implications of eating her partner. She just eats him and moves on. Only humans have these moral dilemmas. Only humans have a voice inside us that competes with the call of natural instinct and tells us when the things we want to do are, or are not, what we really ought to do. That voice, which we call conscience, calls us to live our lives and make our choices with a greater purpose than merely following our immediate desires as the animals do (Romans 2:15). Without this moral sensitivity, our concepts of good and evil, justice and mercy and forgiveness would not exist. Heroes would not exist or villains either. Courage would be impossible. All our best stories and all our noblest actions would be nothing but meaningless nonsense.

We are more than animals. There is a deeper dimension to who we are. There is a reality inside of us that is too intangible to find with a scalpel, yet too powerful to ignore. It shapes our thoughts, our dreams, our sense of justice and purpose, our awareness of beauty, our love and our actions. We were made in the image of God. We were given not only a body but a spirit (Job 32:8). With this gift, God enabled us not only to see and experience the stimuli of the natural world around us (like all creatures do) but also to hear the meaning he communicates through it—to feel the earth quaking with the thunder of God and recognise not only the power but the voice (Psalm 29). With this gift, God enabled us to say something in reply.

Does it make sense now that God gave humans responsibility over his creation? What other creature could represent his justice? What other creature could represent his compassion for all that he has made? What other creature would even notice these things? Humanity has the privilege of expressing God's character on Earth, and we are uniquely equipped to do so. We alone can hear his language, relate to him personally, learn his character and demonstrate it to the rest of his creation. But there's more. The representation can go both ways—not only can we express the glory of God to his creation; we can also express the glorifying praises of creation to our God.

Responding to the One Who Made Us

Psalm 98:8 calls rivers and mountains to praise the Lord: "Let the rivers clap their hands, let the mountains sing together for joy". Isaiah 55:12 says the trees will join in as well, and Psalm 148 adds many more creations to the list—but remember: even though these wonders "pour forth speech" constantly, they "use no words" (Psalm 19:3). While their very existence speaks loudly of the glory of God, there is only one part of creation that can put that declaration into words. It is us. If all of creation is the orchestra of praise, then we are the choir. We are the tongue, the voice of all things, the directors of music, the soloists and singers, the poets and scribes. When we bring our worship to the God of all things, we give vocal expression to the silent language that all things are constantly communicating anyway. In that sense, we are not only speaking for ourselves—we are speaking for an entire universe of wonders. It is a universe that expands far beyond us, and our praise should expand with it.

The orchestra has already begun to play. Are we providing the lyrics? You don't need a fantastic singing voice to join the choir of creation. You can do it right now by simply speaking your thanks and appreciation to God—or at any other moment of any day. There is never an instant, ever, when worship is out of place. As humans, we have the joy of being able to know God and respond personally to him. And what words could we use to respond to a God like this, except words of worship? "Day after day" let us "pour forth speech" (v 2), joining the words of our praise to the constant music of God's creation. "Night after night" let us "reveal knowledge" (v 2) of his character in how we relate to the rest of his created wonders. What a privilege it is to be human.

CHAPTER 16

The Rest of the Story

"You have made us for yourself, O Lord, and our hearts are restless until they find rest in you."

Augustine of Hippo

The early civilisations of Mesopotamia told a story to explain why humans were created. It began with a quarrel between the gods; the minor gods complained to their senior overseers that they were tired of working so hard doing all the menial tasks like growing food and digging canals. They wanted help, and Enki, the most senior of all the gods, responded by creating a substitute to do the work of the gods for them. He made a race of slaves to feed the gods, provide for their needs, and dig their canals: humanity. When the gods saw their new workers, they rejoiced. But did the humans living in Mesopotamia rejoice at such an explanation of their existence?

Today, some tell a different story. They speak of humans as the survivors of a long line of death and destruction. It's called "survival of the fittest", but that's only the positive side. The other side is the death of the weakest, the destruction of the unfit, over and over and over again. Such stories have consequences. What we believe about where we came from determines what we think about why we're here, what it means to be human, what our role is in the world, and how we should live our lives on earth. If we are created as slaves for the gods, then it is vital that we please our masters with the right sacrifices and offerings, or they may destroy us. Many cultures have lived in this way, and a few continue to do so. If, on the other hand, we are merely the lucky beings who survived the chaos of evolution, then the most apparent goal for us to pursue is simply to keep surviving for as long as possible. To achieve this, we must be strong and fit, and never weak. Weakness is the theory of evolution's only sin—strength its only virtue. And yet, no matter how many times we tell ourselves this story, we can never quite bring ourselves to believe it fully. We can never seem to stop valuing the weak or believing that love is more important than raw power, or even survival.

The reason why we can never fully believe such stories is because they are not true. They do not fit with the full reality of who we are. They are misinterpretations of the realities God made and misunderstandings of his purpose in making them. We were not created to be slaves of the gods. We have not evolved for mere survival. Strength is not the only definition of good. We are made in the image of the God who created all things, and we, along with everything else, are made for a good and meaningful purpose. On the seventh day of creation, God gives us a glimpse of this purpose by inventing something quite different from everything he had spoken into existence on the six days before. On the seventh day, God created rest. Rest is not a physical reality like the others, but it is a reality nonetheless, and its placement here at the end of the week of creation shows us that our physical universe is not an end in itself.

Genesis chapter 2 begins with a summary of the first six days of creation, in verse 1: "Thus the heavens and the earth were completed in all their vast array". Completed. So that's the end of the days of creation, right? Not quite. There's one more: "By the seventh day God had finished the work he had been doing; so on the seventh day he rested from all his work. Then God blessed the seventh day and made it holy, because on it he rested from all the work of creating that he had done" (v 2-3).

Discovering and Interpreting Rest

The work of bringing all things into existence was finished. And yet God goes on and adds one more day for rest. If this wasn't so familiar to us, it would definitely be surprising. Does the Creator of galaxies need a break? Does the inventor of the mysterious seas need a siesta? Has the God of everything used up his strength, speaking all of reality into existence? Should we be concerned that this is a possibility? No. The universe proclaims that God's power is as boundless as creation itself and more so. And yet, our boundless God with his boundless power took the seventh day for rest. And he blessed it.

God could have spread his work out over seven days, rather than six—or any other number, for that matter. He could have, but he didn't. He chose the number seven, and he chose to use the last day for rest. From this decision flows the pattern of our seven-day weeks. Later in Scripture, God makes it clear that his people should imitate him in setting one day out of the seven apart. In his Ten Commandments to Old Testament Israel, the fourth is on this topic:

> *Remember the Sabbath day by keeping it holy. Six days you shall labour and do all your work, but the seventh day is a sabbath to the LORD your God. On it you shall not do any work, neither you, nor your son or daughter, nor your male or female servant, nor your animals, nor any foreigner residing in your towns. For in six days the LORD made the heavens and the earth, the sea, and all that is in them, but he rested on the seventh day. Therefore the LORD blessed the Sabbath day and made it holy.* (Exodus 20:8-11)

Clearly, God takes rest very seriously. In the Old Testament, he tells his people that they must rest even when they don't want to: "It is a day of sabbath rest for you, and you must deny yourselves" (Leviticus 23:32). Deny yourselves in order to rest? This sounds backwards to our modern ears, in our world where rest is so often a high priority. For the Israelites, though, a day of rest would take them away from the ongoing work in the fields—a work that would not sit quietly in the inbox until they returned to it. To take a day off was to deny themselves the opportunity of making progress and reaping the rewards that only labour could provide. This is still true today, not only for farmers but for everyone with overflowing diaries and important appointments and more than enough work to fill every spare minute. A whole day of rest every single week is still a kind of a denial. It is a denial of leveraging that time to progress our own plans, our own prosperity, our own position, our own provision. And what is the purpose of this denial?

When God took a day of rest and told his people to do the same, he was teaching them to know, to feel, and to act on the truth that the physical world around them—as vitally important as it has always been—was not actually the point of their existence. The work God gave humanity on Earth is far more significant than we normally realise, and so was God's work of creation. But the work has a goal. A construction site is not successful if it remains a construction site for ever. The goal is a completed building, which can serve its intended purpose—a shop, an office, a church, a home. And when God made creation, he was making a home.

The reason why we so often feel closer to God in nature is because nature is specifically designed to bring us close to God. That's the whole point. Our world was designed to be the physical context for our relationship with him—the four walls of a house that can become so much more. Our home, together. To be at home with God is the definition of true rest. It is not the restless rest of bingeing TV shows and social media. It is not the temporary rest of holidays in the sun. It is not the rest of a happy home or the rest of a long, healthy retirement. This is the complete rest, complete security and complete joy of being close to our Creator. As David wrote:

> You make known to me the path of life;
>   you will fill me with joy in your presence,
>   with eternal pleasures at your right hand.
>   (Psalm 16:11)

For a little while, the world really did work this way when God walked with Adam and Eve in the cool of the evening in the Garden of Eden. All of that changed quickly when Adam and Eve decided that they would be better off on their own, without God. God, however, was not so easily put off. In spite of our sin against him, he continued to draw near. He spoke through his prophets, he provided for his people, he revealed himself in his words and his actions and, when the time was just right, he came to live among us himself—Jesus, Immanuel, God with us.

Responding to Rest

When Jesus came to Earth, he came as the embodiment of rest. He said, "Come to me, all you who are weary and burdened, and I will give you rest. Take my yoke upon you and learn from me, for I am gentle and humble in heart, and you will find rest for your souls. For my yoke is easy and my burden is light" (Matthew 11:28-30). This might sound backwards—isn't a yoke made for working? How can Jesus say, "Take my yoke" in one breath and "You will find rest" in the next? Wouldn't it have been better for him to say, *Take my hammock* or *Take my recliner?* No. I'm not denying that hammocks and recliners are lovely. Ultimately, though, true rest is not a category of activities, or non-activities. True rest is a person. When Jesus says, "I will give you rest", what he means is that he will give us himself. He will take the yoke with us, and with him walking in the yoke beside us, even the heaviest yoke in the world becomes "easy" and any burden at all becomes "light".

God could not save us by lowering the standard of his perfect justice, but through his perfect life, Jesus lifted the yoke for us. Through his death, he took on himself the burden of our sin. Through his resurrection, he won forgiveness and eternal rest for all who trust in him (Hebrews 4:10). This is why Christians traditionally rest on Sundays, because that's the day Jesus rose from the dead and secured our rest for ever. Not only that but he unravelled the curse of creation so that Romans 8:21 could come gloriously true; "That the creation itself will be liberated from its bondage to decay and brought into the freedom and glory of the children of God". So we are not slaves. We are not mere survivors. If we come to Jesus, we are the free children of God himself.

Look at the world around you. Breathe deeply. If you are God's child, then everything you see belongs to your Father. The air you breathe is his air. The trees are his. The birds and the grass and the sun—all his. And he made all of it as a home for you to live in with him. Yes, right now it is a broken home, creaking and groaning (Romans 8:22), but the renovation work has already started in the hearts of his people. The owner is coming to set his house in order. "Do not be afraid, little flock, for your Father has been pleased to give you the kingdom" (Luke 12:32). A new heaven and a new earth are coming, where God will dwell among his people. "They will be his people, and God himself will be with them and be their God. 'He will wipe every tear from their eyes. There will be no more death' or mourning or crying or pain, for the old order of things has passed away" (Revelation 21:3-4).

The purpose of taking a day of rest every week is not simply to recharge and recognise our limitations—although we have those. A day of rest can declare to ourselves, to God, and to the world around us that there is far more to our lives than our physical existence and the things we see and touch. A day of rest can be a picture of God's promise of ultimate rest in Christ, as well as a time for us to intentionally connect with the source of rest himself: our God. In the hectic busyness of modern life, we need this. A weekly day of rest is a gift from God to remind us of what our work and what our world and what our lives are actually for. It is a day to remember where we, and all of creation, are going.

CHAPTER 17

I Wonder as
I Wander

*"Never lose an opportunity of seeing anything
beautiful. Beauty is God's hand-writing—a way-
side sacrament; welcome it in every fair face, every
fair sky, every fair flower, and thank for it Him, the
fountain of all loveliness, and drink it in, simply
and earnestly, with all your eyes; it is a charmed
draught, a cup of blessing."*

Charles Kingsley

I don't usually look very closely at the grass in our
garden although I like having it there. It adds a
pleasing shade of living green that underscores the
roses and herbs, and it feels good under my feet. It
looks great from our windows, especially when the sun
shines. But that kind of looking is just the general kind,
taking in the sweep of everything without noticing the
grass in particular. The only time I consistently focus
on the grass itself is when I'm cutting it—which is a

quick job compared to how long it takes to grow back. "Watching the grass grow" has become an idiom for extreme boredom because it happens so slowly that you can't observe it. It's also just grass, after all—one of the most ordinary, everyday, common forms of life in the world. Yes, it's nice and green and soft underfoot, but if you sit outside and give it your full attention, people will either think you've gone a bit mad or (if they're more charitable) that you've lost a contact lens.

I dare you to sit outside and try it anyway. Sit in the grass, and watch it grow. Give it your full, unhurried attention. Leave your phone inside. Notice it. Soak it in. Notice the shadows it makes in the light of the sun, while that blazing hieroglyph of God's power crosses the sky "like a champion rejoicing to run his course" (Psalm 19:5). Think about the ability God gave to humble, ordinary grass to photosynthesise that sunlight into energy and growth—an expression of dependence on God's provision. If the clouds are concealing the sunlight, consider their ever-changing display of God's glory, or the life-giving water that they give to the grass and all living things, drawn up as it was from the chaotic seas that God rules and uses for our good. Reach down and touch the soil; feel it in your hands and remember God's gift of land and our responsibility to "work it and take care of it" faithfully as his representatives (Genesis 2:15). As your hand moves through the grass, take note if anything stirs—the grass is home to a huge variety of God's creatures. What invisible realities are those creatures sensing that lie beyond your own perception? What do their bodies and sounds and ways of living declare about the God who made them? How do their mandibles, webs or stingers remind you of the way creation groans, longing for restoration? If the grass is mature, consider its seeds. Look at their small size and let them speak to you about God's mysterious gift of life. You can cut the grass in a moment, but only God can make it live and grow. And he set the timetable for that growth, through days and seasons and years, slowly soaking in the sunshine and imperceptibly extending upward day after day, until you sigh and put on the old jeans and come outside to cut it.

I dare you to watch the grass grow and listen carefully to the messages that "pour forth" (Psalm 19:2) from it about God, his gifts, his character, the curse of sin and the way God works in the world and in our lives. (God even compares us to grass in Isaiah 40:6-8.) Watching the grass grow doesn't need to be boring at all once you realise that the growing grass has important things to say to you. As do growing trees and rolling seas and the moss that clings to boulders. The longer you watch and listen to creation, the more you'll hear.

Wander and Wonder

The whole world around you is bursting with meaning and significance—every single detail, every rock and cloud and canyon, every wave, every mushroom, every fox and worm and leaf, everywhere. Watch them all and listen to them all whenever you can, even if it's just while you're walking to your car or looking out of the window. Better yet, spend some time in nature and listen to it "pour forth speech" and "reveal knowledge"

(Psalm 19:2) to you about the one who made it. This world was made for wandering, and your soul was made for wonder. Every corner of our planet speaks differently, and you have the privilege, right now, of being alive and able to hear it. Don't rush that. Don't hurry through this world as if it were just the painted backdrop of a photo booth. Slow down. Pay attention.

Let your wonder grow as you wander through a forest or climb a mountain or let the never-ending current push your kayak down a river. Turn the soil, plant some seeds, and see what God has to say to you through the seasons of their growth. Pitch a tent in the wilderness and listen to the distinctive sounds of the night. Look up at the sky in the morning, not just to assess the weather but to refresh your soul in your Creator. Watch the path of a bumblebee, consider the weed pushing through concrete, notice the houseplant bending towards the light—and bend your own heart towards the Light of the world. Wherever you go and whatever you do, keep your eyes and ears open to hear and your heart ready to respond to the voice of God in all that he has made.

You don't have to wait for a chance to visit the world's most exotic places or unravel its deepest mysteries. Beauty spots and groundbreaking discoveries are wonderful, and it's good to seek them out, but don't overlook the fact that you have more than enough to wonder at right in front of you, right now. It's easy to forget to notice the grass growing under your feet or the many other created hieroglyphs all around you, all the time. Somehow, when we see things often, we tend to see them less clearly. Imagine if you only ever saw one songbird or one daffodil or one rainbow in your whole life—wouldn't you be overwhelmed by it? So why are we not overwhelmed when we've seen a thousand? It takes work to keep your eyes open and think about what is actually in front of you, instead of letting it all fade into the invisibility of the ordinary.

Ordinary! Is there really such a thing? It seems to me the only reason we have that word at all is because God filled his universe with too many wonders for us to comprehend. Have you seen the way the sun shines through the leaves or shimmers across the water? Have you considered the order and efficiency displayed in each individual living cell? Have you held a baby? Have you wondered at your ability to wonder or lost yourself in the beauty of the dawn chorus? The fact that God is so generous with his creative marvels does not make them less amazing, even if the abundance makes us less amazed (which is odd, isn't it?). When God does something awe-inspiring one time, we call it a miracle. When he does it a billion times, we call it ordinary. Look a little closer, and you'll see that "ordinary" is just another word for the miracles God decided to repeat. And he repeats them on purpose—the natural world is overflowing all around us with a constant stream of God's language, with never-ending messages from our Creator.

If you don't understand a particular aspect of creation or what God could be saying to you through it, you can ask him for help and seek answers. He revealed himself to you in two languages—his created world and written word—because he genuinely wants you to know him. He promised that his own Holy Spirit would guide his people to the truth (John 16:13). He revealed himself supremely in his Son, who is "the radiance of God's glory and the exact representation of his being" (Hebrews 1:3). God wants to be known. He wants you to draw near to him.

Wonder And Worship
God filled his world with hieroglyphics that live and grow, that burn and shine, that echo and roar and sing. Truly, we live in a world of wonders. Yet the greatest wonder of all is the Author who wrote them. Every marvellous, glorious creation in the universe is a tantalising taste, a faint reflection of the immeasurable glory of the Maker of all things—"These are but the outer fringe of his works; how faint the whisper we hear of him! Who then can understand the thunder of his power?" (Job 26:14). The innumerable, expanding galaxies declare every night that the glory of their Maker is more limitless than the entire universe he made, though they do it without a voice and without words (Psalm 19:1-3).

You have the words. You have the voice. And you can join your voice to the symphony of all things and declare with all of creation the excellence of God's wisdom (Psalm 104:24), his power (Jeremiah 32:17), his love and provision and goodness and patience and attention to detail and creativity and faithfulness. And not only can you declare these things about God; you can reply directly to him—you can speak to the one who is constantly speaking to you. You can answer his invitation and draw near to him. You can respond to his voice. All of creation is speaking. Will you?

Psalm 148

Praise the LORD.

Praise the LORD from the heavens;
* praise him in the heights above.*
Praise him, all his angels;
* praise him, all his heavenly hosts.*
Praise him, sun and moon;
* praise him, all you shining stars.*
Praise him, you highest heavens
* and you waters above the skies.*

Let them praise the name of the LORD,
* for at his command they were created,*
and he established them for ever and ever—
* he issued a decree that will never pass away.*

Praise the LORD from the earth,
* you great sea creatures and all ocean depths,*
lightning and hail, snow and clouds,
* stormy winds that do his bidding,*
you mountains and all hills,
* fruit trees and all cedars,*
wild animals and all cattle,
* small creatures and flying birds,*
kings of the earth and all nations,
* you princes and all rulers on earth,*
young men and women,
* old men and children.*

Let them praise the name of the LORD,
  for his name alone is exalted;
  his splendour is above the earth and the heavens.
And he has raised up for his people a horn,
  the praise of all his faithful servants,
  of Israel, the people close to his heart.

Praise the LORD.

Also by Seth Lewis

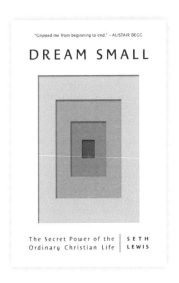

The world tells us that significance comes from dreaming big and making a big impact. This book reminds us that when we know Jesus, we are free from the world's definition of success. It's a celebration of dreaming small: of finding significance through service, investing in individuals, being faithful in small things and finding our value in Christ.

thegoodbook.com/dream-small

thegoodbook.co.uk/dream-small

thegoodbook.com.au/dream-small

Embracing the Limits of
Where and When God Has You

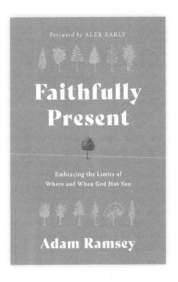

Often we're so busy thinking about the next thing that we're at risk of missing the main thing: the people and places God has put in front of us, right here, right now. There is a better way to live. In this thought-provoking book, readers will discover fresh joy in the little things, freedom from the tyranny of time and contentment in every season of life.

thegoodbook.com/present

thegoodbook.co.uk/present

thegoodbook.com.au/present

Seeing the Fruit of the Spirit through Story and Scripture

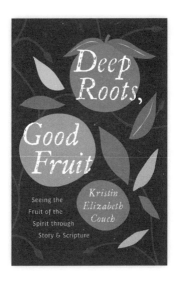

What does the fruit of the Spirit look like in everyday life? By combining captivating stories with rich meditations on Scripture, Kristin Elizabeth Couch encourages us to see that God is at work even in life's mundane moments, and that although our growth may seem slow, in the Spirit's power we really can become more like Jesus.

thegoodbook.com/good-fruit

thegoodbook.co.uk/good-fruit

thegoodbook.com.au/good-fruit

COMPANY

BIBLICAL | RELEVANT | ACCESSIBLE

At The Good Book Company we are dedicated to helping Christians and local churches grow. We believe that God's growth process always starts with hearing clearly what he has said to us through his timeless and flawless word—the Bible.

Ever since we opened our doors in 1991, we have been striving to produce resources that are biblical, relevant, and accessible. By God's grace, we have grown to become an international publisher, encouraging ordinary Christians of every age and stage and every background and denomination to live for Christ day by day and equipping churches to grow in their knowledge of God, their love for one another, and the effectiveness of their outreach.

Call one of our friendly team for a discussion of your needs or visit one of our local websites for more information on the resources and services we provide.

Your friends at The Good Book Company

thegoodbook.com | thegoodbook.co.uk
thegoodbook.com.au | thegoodbook.co.nz
thegoodbook.co.in